Safe Photo Etching for Photographers and Artists

Thomas J. Lipton Inc. is proud to sponsor this first printing of the Canadian publication "Safe Photo Etching for Photographers and Artists". In so doing we acknowledge the importance of presenting new non-toxic etching processes that are environmentally safer than processes currently in use.

The safe and innovative etching techniques outlined in this publication will give artists a new sense of creative freedom that will ultimately lead to a unique body of art work, which in turn, will enrich us all.

For Kath —
Good Printmaking Safely
Keith Howard

About The Author

Keith Howard was born in Australia and has an undergraduate degree, majoring in painting, from The National Art School, East Sydney Technical College, Australia; a post graduate degree in education from Sydney Teachers College, Australia and a masters degree in studio art from New York University, U.S.A.

He is a practicing artist/printmaker whose prints have been shown in over 40 international juried print exhibitions and is represented in many collections world-wide. Presently his art work is sold through the following dealers: Geraldine Davis Gallery, Toronto, Canada; La Guilde Graphic, Montreal, Canada; Prior Editions, Vancouver, Canada; Artvest, Brisbane, Australia.

For the past 17 years he has taught in art colleges and universities in both Canada and Australia, specializing in printmaking, photography and drawing. He has given many demonstrations and workshops to art colleges, universities, arts organizations and professional printmaking organization on the "Howard Process" and, in the interest of promoting safe printmaking practices, will continue to do so. Any inquiries regarding demonstrations or workshops of the "Howard Process" should be addressed to the publisher or to :

Keith Howard
Visual Arts Instructor
Grande Prairie Regional College
10726-106 Ave.
Grande Prairie
Alberta T8V 4C4
Canada

The "Howard Process", as described in this book, is not a definitive process. There is still a great deal of experimenting to be done. Any artist/ photographer who discovers new and innovative applications of the "Howard Process" is invited to share this information by contacting the author at the above address. Any original contribution, used in future publication, will be fully acknowledged.

Above: Keith Howard demonstraing the hard ground coating method at the "Howard Process" workshop given at the Honolulu Academy of Arts, Hawaii, July 5, 1991.

Above: Keith Howard during a lecture on the "Howard Process" at the South Australia School of Art, June 21, 1991, in Adelaide, Australia.

Above: Keith Howard (far right) addressing staff and students at the "Howard Process" workshop conducted at the University of New South Wales, May 20, 1991 in Sydney, Australia.

Safe Photo Etching for Photographers and Artists

Includes a complete guide to making etchings,10 innovative hand etching techniques and the "Howard Process"

By Keith Howard

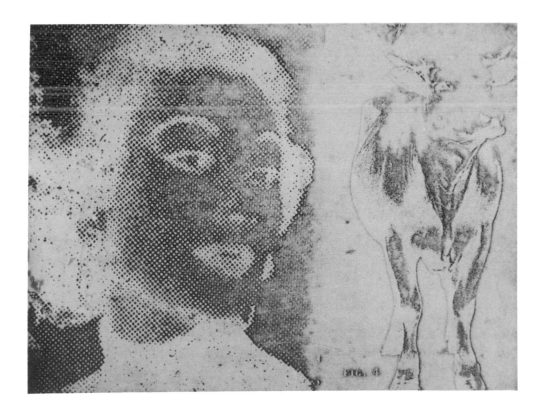

Larry Parkinson, photo etching, 6" x 8". This etching was made at the "Howard Process" workshop at the Australian Print Workshop, Melbourne, Australia on June 28, 1991.

Dedicated to my wife Rhonda and son Harrison.

All etchings and photographs used to illustrate the
text are by the author unless otherwise noted.

Book designed by the author.

KNOX is a registered trademark and used
with the permission of Thomas J. Lipton Inc.

Inquiries should be addressed to:

The Editor
Wynne Resources
P.O. Box 7587
Peace River
Alberta T8S 1T2
Canada
Phone (403) 624-5566
FAX (403) 624-3344

Also published in Australia by:

Artvest Australia
G. P. O. Box 1770
Brisbane
Queensland 4001
Australia
Phone (07) 358-5156
Australian ISBN: 0-646-06601-3

North American ISBN: 0-9695577-0-1

Canadian Cataloguing in Publication Data

Howard, Keith (Keith John)
Safe photo etching for photographers and artists
Includes index.
ISBN 0-9695577-0-1

1. Photoengraving--Technique.   2. Photography--Technique
3. Prints--Technique. 4. Etching--Technique.   I. Title.
TR970.H69 1991   686.2'327   C91-091816-3

Acknowledgements

Deli Sacilotto is one of the great innovative printmakers of the past two decades and has been an inspiration to me. It was indirectly through his book, "Photographic Printmaking Techniques", that I discovered the foundation for my present area of enquiry.

To my good friend Larry Fletcher, a printmaker from Dixonville, Alberta, who has been indispensable in his dedication in helping me demonstrate all of the processes in this book for my camera and in addition has been invaluable in the preliminary editing process.

The editing process of this book has been through the hands of my wife Rhonda Howard, my colleagues Barb Duffy Tagg and Erna Luger and finally to Patricia Adamson, who's dedication to the proofing task needs special mention. Their input and help have been of great assistance to me.

To Victoria Edgar and Alain Costaz of La Guilde Graphic in Montreal and Montreal printmaker Wendy Simon who have shown extraordinary creativity in the utilization of the "Howard Process".

A special thanks to Harold and Joan Wynne of Wynne Resources for their great courage, insights, creative energy and for having faith in me.

To, Biagio Mariorino, Ken Burkholder, Blaine Ruttan, John Stewart, Joann Murdock, Roslyn de Mille, Alan Mann, Jo Wilson, Joanne Kardaras, Larry Parkinson, David Gafiss and Barbara McSween who have also utilized the "Howard Process" in their own prints and in doing so have made an important contribution to the content of this book.

To all my students who have been a constant source of moral support.

To Grande Prairie Regional College and especially to the staff in the Visual and Performing Arts Department for their encouragement and support.

To Alan Koval, Tamara Steele and Kristi Knowles from Thomas J. Lipton Inc. who have supported my research and workshops by donating generous quantities of Knox Gelatine. I wish also to thank them for their extended efforts and acumen that resulted in their company sponsoring this first Canadian publication.

To Lisa McLean, director of the Malaspina Printmakers Society in Vancouver, who had the foresight and conviction to sponsor the first "Howard Process" workshop in July of 1989.

To Bill Blundell who wrote to me on November 25, 1989 with the following advice. "Future acrylic floor polish makes an excellent hard-ground and is great for covering up marks and pinholes". This advice has promoted a completely new area of enquiry within this book.

To Pat Bach, Marj Lubbers and Gina Albert have been very supportive in lending me a word processing computer and teaching me how to use it.

This acknowledgement would not be complete without thanking my wife Rhonda for supporting me through the lengthy, and at times frustrating, process of writing this book.

Contents

Contents

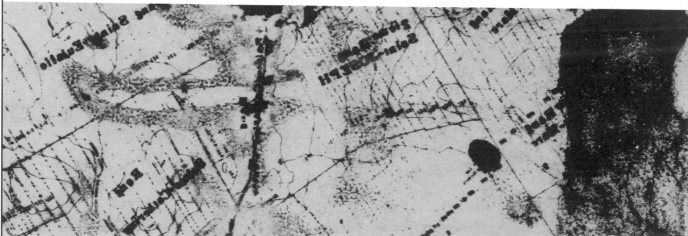

Victoria Edgar, "At Home", etching, 12" x 12", utilizing the "Howard Process". This etching was made with a combination of a photocopy map of Montreal, aquatint and hand drawn stencils. The **insert** is a 3 times enlargement of a small part of "AT Home" showing the fineness of detail possible when the "Howard Process" is utilized for photo etching..

Preface to the "Howard Process"

All commercial photo-mechanical methods of reproduction were designed primarily for the purpose of faithfully reproducing a photograph. The "Howard Process" is the first process that has been designed specifically for a duality of purpose. In the first instance it has the ability to faithfully reproduce a photograph; in the second, it has the ability to abstract and interpret from the photograph in such a manner ideally suited to the creative demands of the artist. Also, as it is derived from the very first method of photo reproduction and uses the most modern technologies, it is both the most traditional and most modern of photo etching techniques.

The techniques outlined in this book are meant as a starting process to initiate further creative exploration of the "Howard Process".

When first reading this book it is important to ascertain which portion of this text is most pertinent to your needs.

The **"Howard Process" begins at page 23** with the section **"Stock Sensitizing Solution"**. If your sole intention is to learn about this process you should begin there. Pages 23 through to 62 deal with the "Howard Process" in its entirety including specialized equipment you will have to construct for your studio or class room.

Pages 5 through to 18 have been especially compiled for those who are interested in the **photographic side** of the "Howard Process". These pages outline the steps necessary in making halftones. I have made every endeavour to simplify the procedure for making good in-house halftones but the problem of making good halftones existed before I developed the "Howard Process" and still exists. In fact this is one of the most difficult aspects of making photo etchings. For those readers who have no particular interest in this photo-mechanical process it is possible to achieve similar halftones by taking a photograph to your local photocopy center and asking them to make an 85 line halftone photocopy onto acetate.

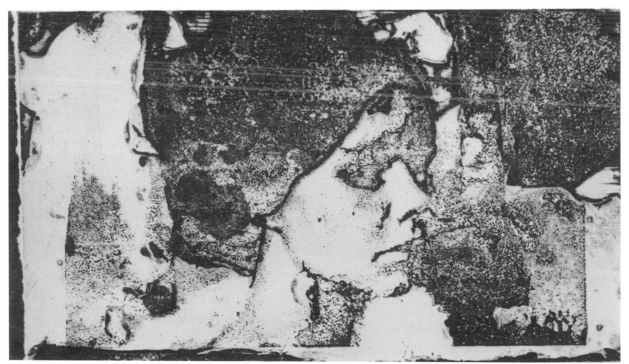

Wendy Simon, Trial Proof of an etching, 8.5" x 5". Utilizing the "Howard Process". That was made from a Kodalith positive produced from a black and white negative. This plate was not aquatinted. The resulting texture and disintegration of the image was due to developing the Kodalith positive in fine line developer and partially etching the plate (during the final stage) in a watered down ferric chloride solution. This is a perfect example of how the "Howard Process" can be creatively manipulated to suit the individual artist image demands.

Introduction

The original aim, when first writing this book, was to elaborate on the "Howard Process" which is a new, safe and simple water based photo etching process. However, during the course of experimentation and investigations into the "Howard Process" I made a few unique discoveries that further expanded the field of hand etching processes. That, coupled with developing a new approach to making halftones and supplying enough information to enable anyone to be able to pick up this book and successfully complete an etching, led to this more comprehensive book.

The information contained in this book will allow the artist a new flexibility and freedom to pursue etching at a safe, simple and inexpensive level never dreamed of before. Anyone involved in printmaking, from the high school, art college or university level to the artist, printmaker and photographer, would benefit from the information documented in this book.

The development of the "Howard Process" was born out of the frustration I experienced with alternative photo printmaking processes. These processes were either expensive, requiring the use of acids and toxic chemicals, or were time consuming, difficult and technically complex.

Due to health concerns, artists and art educators have become increasingly aware of the occupational hazards associated with their art processes. One of the major motivating forces behind the development of this new process was the need to make the studio and class room a healthier and safer place in which to work. With this in mind, I researched most of the currently used photo etching processes in an effort to find a technique that would satisfy the following criteria:

1. Present the lowest health and safety risk.

2. Have the ability to produce a full range of tonal values.

3. Exhibit a degree of technical simplicity and predictability.

4. Be as inexpensive as possible.

5. Use products that are readily available.

This seemed like a tall order to fill. The process that came closest to satisfying these aims was photogravure. Sacilotto's book, "Photographic Printmaking Techniques", proved to be an invaluable source of information on photogravure.

The technique of photogravure, as described in Sacilotto's book, has proven to be very successful but, as the author concedes, is also one of the most complex. This technique used a light-sensitive gelatin-coated paper called carbon tissue as the photo emulsion. The optimum workability of this carbon tissue relied upon the atmospheric humidity being at the ideal level of 60%. This was an aggravating stumbling block for me as I was working in an environment that was very dry for most of the year.

The logical alternative, I felt, was to do away with the carbon tissue and replace it with a liquid gelatin emulsion.

I did my first experiment in October 1988 using unflavoured Knox Gelatine purchased from a local supermarket. Since that time this process has matured and developed into a unique and diverse process.

Since August of 1989 I have been giving demonstrations and workshops on the "Howard Process", and the ensuing response has been overwhelming. Several newspaper articles and Printmaking Societies newsletters have published articles on the process. Printmakers and photographers from all over the world have contacted me requesting more information and have sent me samples of unflavoured gelatin (available in their local supermarket) to test the "Howard Process". (So far every sample has worked well.) This book is a response to their request to provide more detailed information on the "Howard Process".

The information contained in this book is a guide on "how to" creatively use and manipulate this new photo etching process and introduces some completely new nonphoto techniques. It also offers safe alternatives to most traditional etching techniques.

What is a Photo Etching?

Etching: the Process

The process of etching dates from the 15th century. It involved coating a metal plate with a thin, acid resisting emulsion. This emulsion, when dry, was then drawn upon with a finely pointed instrument. Enough pressure was used to break the emulsion surface, thus exposing the metal underneath. The exposed metal was then etched with an acid or mordant to create finely incised lines. After the metal plate had enough incised lines to create an image, it was etched, inked, wiped and printed. Thus a metal plate that had been etched in such a manner could produce many identical images.

Above: Drawing through the acid resisting coating.

The Photo Etching

It was not until the 19th century, with the invention of photography, that Niepce and Talbot first developed techniques for making photo etchings.

The difference between the etching process previously described and photo etching lies in the nature of the acid resistant coating. The coating used in photo etching is sensitive to ultraviolet light. When a piece of photographic film is placed on top of this sensitized etching plate and exposed to an ultraviolet light, a change in the emulsion occurs. Because the photographic film is composed of opaque and transparent areas, this sensitized emulsion is selectively exposed. The parts of the plate that were exposed to the ultraviolet light harden, providing an acid resistant surface. The parts of the plate that were unexposed are washed away with water or special developer, revealing the metal underneath. This metal is eventually attacked by the acid or mordant to produce the photo etching plate.

Above : Removing the etching from the plate after being pressed in the etching press.

An Historical Perspective

Photogravure and Photography

In 1852 Henry Fox Talbot first developed the process known as photogravure. This involved coating a copper plate with a thin layer of sensitized colloid gelatin and etching it in platinic chloride. Later developments included the use of a rosin aquatint and substituting platinic chloride with ferric chloride.

Photogravure then went through two further stages of refinement. The first was by Joseph Swann who in 1864 invented the carbon tissue. This was a heavily-pigmented, gelatin-coated paper which facilitated the transfer of the photograph to the copper plate. The second was by Karl Klick who shortly after developed a special halftone screen. These later innovations propelled photogravure into the commercial printing industry that became known as "Rotogravure".

The invention of photography in 1839 and the subsequent development of photogravure became a bipartisan threat to the artist. Previously the artist held the monopoly on pictorial expression.

In 1867 a group of French artists, including Calametta, Henriquel-Dupont and Celestin Nanteuil, proclaimed, "Photography consists of a series of entirely manual operations...... .....the resulting prints can in no way be likened to works born of intellectual effort and artistic study." These sentiments have influenced artistic consciousness, relative to the artistic application of photography, up until the middle of the 20th century.

In the 1960's an innovative group of New York painters openly embraced photographic imagery and its symbiotic relationship to the commercial printing process as part of their artistic expression.

To some degree, it was these painters that liberated the printmaker from the confines of tradition, making photo imagery and the new technical processes a more legitimate tool in their image making arsenal.

The art school was to be the last bastion for maintaining traditional values in art. Photography and photo printmaking trod a parallel path and slowly, since the 1970's, have gained in artistic acceptability and importance.

Notable artists such as Jasper Johns, Robert Rauschenberg, James Rosenquist, Roy Lichtenstein and Andy Warhol utilized these new photo-mechanical technologies with creative gusto and so, too, have many other artists.

In the ensuing wake of discovery the dormant possibilities of photography rose like the Phoenix and became liberated from the traditional stigma of artistic inferiority. One important aspect of this pictorial revolution went virtually unnoticed: the adverse health effects these new photo-mechanical technologies were having on the artists. The net result has been a generation of artists that have suffered ill effects because of exposure to hazardous occupational chemicals.

During the years between first employment of these technologies until recently, when they were proven to be injurious to our health, artist/printmakers have unfortunately grown dependent on them. They were forced to choose between permanently damaging their health, revising the manner in which they worked, exclusively utilizing traditional methods or giving up the use of these new processes. Because photography has become such an integral part of modern art, reverting back to traditional methods is an ideological amputation that most artists are not prepared to endure.

One logical alternative was to revise the manner in which artists worked by following recognized safety procedures and renovating printmaking studios to exhaust dangerous fumes. Because of the additional costs and inconvenience involved, this is easier said than done.

Many artists have resigned themselves to the hazards, doing whatever they can in their particular circumstances to safeguard their health.

One of the most widely known light-sensitive emulsions utilized in photo etching is **KPR** (Kodak Photo Resist). This product and its developer have a high concentrate of methyl cellosolve acetate and xylene. Xylene is a **central nervous system depressant, a skin irritant, defatting agent, an irritant to the mucous membranes** and is absorbed through the skin. Methyl cellosolve acetate is also easily absorbed through the skin and can cause **liver, kidney and brain damage.** As well, the subsequent acids used to etch the metal plate carrying the emulsion can cause **irreversible lung damage.**

Some artists believe that wearing protective gloves and an organic-filtered respirator is sufficient safeguard when using K.P.R and its developer. Because these chemicals are absorbed through exposed skin a completely sealed chemical resistant suit and external breathing apparatus is the only true safeguard.

Literature pertaining to health and safety for the artist has been widespread and relatively easy to obtain. Why then, in the face of this overwhelming evidence, do artists continue to put themselves at risk? The reasons relate to the familiarity with the K.P.R. medium and to a definite lack of viable alternatives.

This book addresses the above concern by offering an alternate photo etching process that is relatively simple, yields optimum results, and is unquestionably one of the safest methods known.

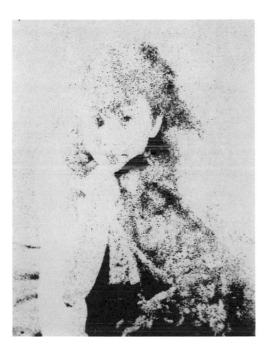

Above: Etching, 9" x 12", by Blaine Ruttan, utilizing the spray coating method on page 40. The plate, for this etching, was spray-coated, exposed to an 85 line halftone image of the photograph on the right and etched for 3 hours in 42 Baume ferric chloride. This was the first print made directly after the plate was etched.

Above: Photograph by Blaine Ruttan.

The spray coating method of the "Howard Process" is the first photo etching process to allow the artist the freedom to abstract from the original photographic source.

What is a "Halftone Photograph"?

Photographs published in newspapers or on advertising billboards all have one thing in common: They have been transformed into a series of dots to facilitate the commercial printing processes used. Most of the time, however, these dots are not readily noticeable.

In black and white reproductions these dots denote the numerous tonalities between black and white by the number of black dots to cluster together. The white areas have very few to no dots and the black areas have the highest concentration. In colour reproductions, cyan, yellow, magenta and black dots are clustered together in various combinations to express the various colour separations.

The technology for making a black and white halftone photograph is relatively simple and it is this technique that enables artists to make full tonal etchings.

Above: An 85 line elliptical dot halftone image.

Above: A coarse mezzotint halftone image.

The Halftone Screen and Lith Film

Originally, the halftone screen was made from glass that had very fine lines ruled in a regular grid onto one surface. Today the glass has been replaced by a flexible acetate film and is more commonly known as the contact screen. The contact screen can be purchased in varying dot styles and sizes.

For the process described in this book, the best screens are either the 85 line elliptical dot halftone screen, or the coarse mezzotint halftone screen. The 85 line denotation refers to the number of possible dots printed per inch. It is possible to buy screens that produce from as few as 45 dots to the inch to ones that produce 500 dots to the inch. The screen used for newspaper reproductions is generally the 85 line screen. There are many different types of screens, and the principle for using each is the same for all. The results will differ between screens and **exploring the differences** could prove to be beneficial. The local photographic equipment accessory store or off-set printer could give further advice.

The **lith film** is the vehicle for transferring the photograph to the etching plate. This film has an acetate base that is coated with a light-sensitive coating similar to, but not as sensitive as, the black and white film used in 35 mm cameras. If a 35 mm black and white negative was projected directly on to this film, the resulting image would be a black film positive devoid of any intermittent grey tonality, somewhat similar to a high contrast photograph. This is known as either a "**line shot**", "**line image**", or "**tone dropout**". There is a method of utilizing this type of high contrast image that I will be dealing with on page 15.

If a black and white negative is enlarged onto the lith film through a halftone screen, the resulting positive will have a full tonal scale composed of various sized dots formed as a result of the interposing halftone screen.

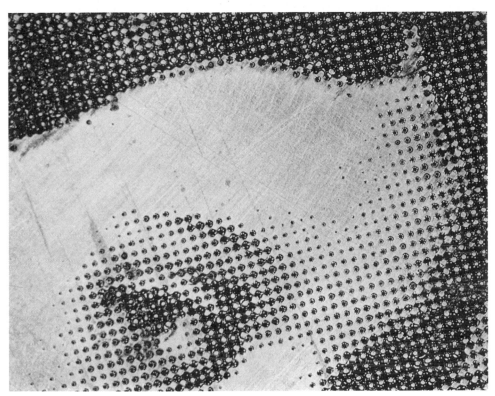

Above: An 10 X magnification of an inked-up etching plate.

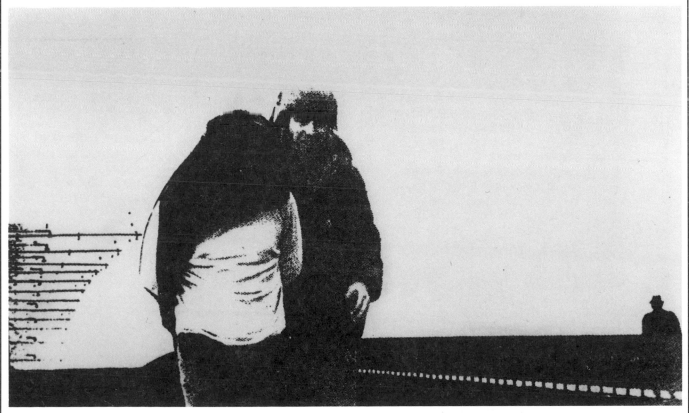

Above: Photo etching, 9" x 5" by Alain Costaz. This photo etching utilized the "Howard Process" with an 85 line half tone screen.

The Darkroom Setup

The photographic darkroom is simply what the name implies. It is a room which permits complete control of the light source from white light to total darkness for the purpose of making photographs. This room should have independent dual-light sources to give white or red light. Hot and cold running water, a sink and lots of table space are also indispensable.

The average bathroom can be temporarily converted into a darkroom by covering the door cracks and window with black plastic purchased from the hardware store. Plans for building more professional darkrooms can be found in the reference books listed, under photography, in the "Selected Reading" section on page 106.

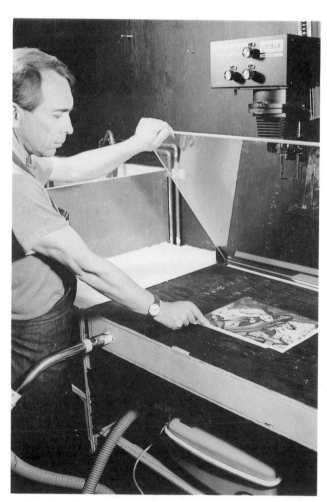

Above: The enlarger with home made vacuum table.

Darkroom Setup

The following basic equipment and materials will be needed:

1. Enlarger.

2. An enlarging base table with vacuum bed.

3. Developer, stop, fixer and washout trays.

4. Halftone screen.

5. Lith film.

6. Lith film developer, fixer and stop solution.

7. Running water.

8. Measuring beakers.

The Enlarger

An enlarger is a device that projects light through a photographic negative via a lens in such a way as to enlarge the negative image, through this projection of light, onto the baseboard of the enlarger.

There are two types of enlargers; one used for colour photography and the other used for black and white photography. Either enlarger can make halftones. Generally, when first starting out, budget is of prime concern. One of the least expensive alternatives is to track down a secondhand black and white enlarger. A secondhand colour-head enlarger will probably cost more but has greater diversity of use, especially if enlargements are to be made onto multigrade black and white photographic paper. The quality of the enlarging lens will be reflected in the finished print. Before considering purchasing a secondhand enlarger, become familiar with the variety of enlargers and accessories that are available. This can be done through the study of photographic books or by questioning the sales people at the local photographic equipment store.

The Vacuum Table

A vacuum table is important if good quality halftones are to be made. One method is to build a box approximately 36" long, 28" wide, and 4" deep. The top face of this box is drilled with a 32nd of an inch hole every square inch, and a large hole drilled in the side to accommodate the vacuum hose. An ordinary household vacuum cleaner will suffice. This will also need a glass lid. (see diagram)

An alternative to the vacuum frame is to build a hinged glass frame that closes down onto a pad of foam rubber that can be locked into place with latches. (see diagram)

The Developing Trays

The size of the etching you intend working on will dictate the size of your trays. You will need at least four trays. The first is for the developer, the second for the stop bath, the third for the fixer and the fourth for the wash bath. Plastic photo trays are readily available in a number of sizes at your local photo supply store.

Other Darkroom Accessories

The following darkroom accessories are recommended :

1. Darkroom thermometer.

2. Two (one-litre size) measuring beakers.

3. Film developing tank. If development of 35mm black and white film is to be carried out, the plastic Patterson tank is one of the easiest to use.

4. Some sort of drying rack or a makeshift clothes line with wooden clothes pegs.

5. Darkroom timer.

6. Focus-scope, (an enlarger focusing aid).

7. Darkroom tongs.

8. Paper and film squeegee.

Above: A foam padded exposure unit utilizing sunlight to expose a plate.

Above: Foam padded exposure table with glass lid open.

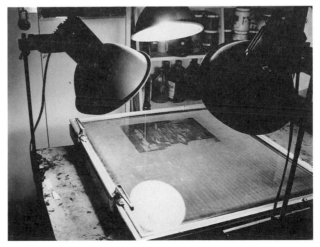

Above: A commercially made vacuum frame utilizing three B.C.A. 115-120V G.E. photo floodlights as the exposure source.

How to Make the Perfect Halftone

Halftones vary in dot structure according to the printmaking technique used. In photo **screenprinting**, the blackest area of the positive halftone to be printed will have dots that are so closely packed that it looks completely black. The black dot can "fill in" and will work perfectly. On the other hand, the blackest area of the positive halftone to be used in **photo etching,** because of the nature of the intaglio printing process, (see page 63) must have some dots. When making halftone positives, the dot structure must be keenly observed. Radio Shack Canadian stores have available an inexpensive 30X power pocket microscope called the Micronta 30X (cat. no. 63-851) which is ideal for examining dot structure. There are many other different magnifiers that magnify 8X power and up to serve the same purpose (see page 95 and 96).

Darkroom Materials

1. Lith film.
If the local photo supply store does not carry this type of graphic arts film, they should be able to give advice as to other sources of supply. Lith film is made by a number of leading film manufacturers.

Kodak's brand name for this film is Kodalith; Fuji is Fujilith; Ilford's is Ilfolith; Dupont calls their film Select Line Film.

Lith film varies in size, quantity, price, quality, and packaging (roll or pre-cut sheets). Choose the one that will best suit the task at hand. I have found Dupont film to be one of the least expensive.

2. Lith film special two-part developer.
Again, each company that sells this type of film will sell its own special developer generally packaged as part A and part B, in either a liquid or powdered concentrate.

The Kodalith Liquid developer in the liquid concentrate makes up to 20 gallons and is one of the most economical. (If a 20 gallon container is purchased, buy the screw-on dispensing units for easy pouring.)

3. Stop bath.
This can be easily made by mixing acetic acid (white vinegar) and water. Mix 1 part of vinegar to 20 parts water.

4. Film fixer
The last chemical to be mixed is the **film fixer.** Again, each manufacturer makes their own brand. Kodak Rapid Fixer, made up from the liquid concentrate is one of the most economical.

Darkroom Procedure

Organizational skills are an important part of making halftones. Devise an efficient and economical way of working within the confines of the darkroom. Allocate a space for each of the component parts of the operation and make sure there is no conflict between these spaces. Divide the darkroom into a *wet* handling side and a *dry* handling side and be sure to maintain this separation through every procedure.

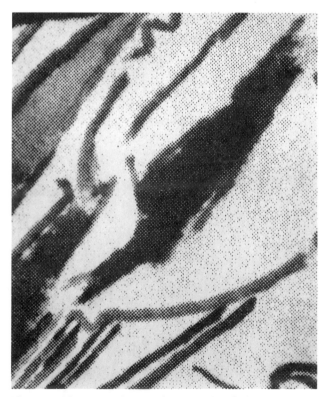

Above: Close-up (magnified 30X) of the blackest area of a halftone etching.

Making the Halftone

The process involves placing a black and white negative in the enlarger and projecting the image through the halftone screen onto the lith film. This film is then developed, placed into a stop bath, then placed into a fixing bath and finally washed in water and hung up to dry.

This sounds easy enough but it is not quite that simple, as it is necessary to give the lith film **two separate exposures.**

The first is done with the halftone screen in contact with the film. This is called **the main exposure.**

The second exposure is done without the halftone screen and this is called **the shadow detail exposure.**

Before elaborating on these procedures, I must outline four critical aspects to making successful halftones:

1. It is vital to accurately time each step of the procedure, especially the exposure and development times.

2. Limit the development time to 3 minutes. During this 3 minute period the developing tray should be rocked back and forth for the first 1.5 minutes. During the remaining 1.5 minutes, the developer should be left still.

3. The third and most important point is to discard the developer 20 to 30 minutes after it is mixed as this solution weakens, resulting in an inability to accurately predict the outcome of the developing process. **To maintain consistently good results it is very important to accurately and methodically time each step of the process.**

4. The temperature of developer, stop bath, fix and water wash should be between 68°F and 70°F. It is important to be consistent, especially with respect to the temperature of the developer.

Lith Film Exposure

The main variables when trying to determine the correct exposure for the lith film are:

1. The distance the enlarger is from its own baseboard.

2. The type of enlarger light source.

3. The density of your negative.

4. The aperture of the enlarger lens.

There is only one optimum exposure, and the best way to determine this is by making small test strips of lith film and exposing them separately.

Above: A strip of negatives showing different densities.

Above: Adjusting the aperture of the enlarging lens.

Making the Test Strip

Making the **test strip** is the prelude to making the finished halftone positive. This procedure is carried out under a **red** safelight as follows:

1. **Below:** Place the negative, emulsion (dull side) down into the negative carrier of the enlarger. Project the negative onto the vacuum baseboard to focus and size up. Place tape onto the baseboard to indicate the perimeter of the enlarged image size.

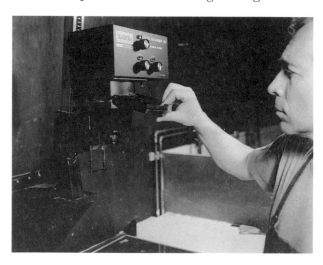

2. Position a strip of lith film, approx. 6"x 6", onto the baseboard in such a manner so it intrudes into the lightest area of the projected image. As the image projected is a negative, the lightest area will be the area on the baseboard with the least amount of light. (This may seem a contradiction of terms but we are dealing with a **negative** image rather than a positive.)

Below: The strip of lith film should be taped down to the baseboard at one edge.

3. The aperture of the enlarger lens is designed to control the amount of light passing through the negative to the baseboard. This is one of the exposure variables previously mentioned. Adapt an aperture that suits the particular negative and image size being used. It may be necessary, for instance, to open the aperture up to F4 when making a large blow-up, and conversely it may be necessary to close the aperture down to F22 when making a small blow-up. For the purpose of this explanation an aperture of F8 is used.

4. Place the halftone screen on top of the test piece of lith film. Make sure the emulsion side (the side of the film that appears to be the lightest) is facing up and the emulsion side of the contact screen is facing down. The contact screen will have directions as to its emulsion side and to its proper use.

5. **Above:** Close the glass lid and start vacuum.

6. How long should this test strip of lith film be exposed? Again, there are many variables, such as **negative density, light source, distance light source is from the baseboard, aperture, and type of halftone screen.** When starting out, many test strips may be necessary until familiarization is achieved.

For the sake of this explanation, time increments of 2 seconds will be used.

Below: The enlarger timer is set at 2 seconds and the entire piece of lith film is exposed for this time. Then a piece of light blocking card is placed on top of this test piece of film, so as to cover up approximately one third of the film area. The enlarger lamp is turned on for another 2 seconds, and the card shifted to cover up two thirds of the area. A further 2 second exposure is given. This test piece of film has now had three exposures at 2, 4, and 6 seconds respectively.

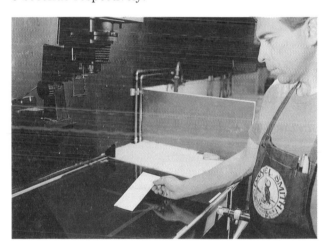

7. As this first test is to determine the **main exposure**, the test film is removed from the baseboard, placed into the developer and agitated for exactly 1.5 minutes, then left for a further 1.5 minutes without agitation. Use a darkroom timer to time this procedure.

After development, place film into stop bath for about 30 seconds and then into fixer, until the lighter areas of the film turn transparent.

After a short wash, squeegee the excess water off the film.

Below: The film is now ready for close scrutiny with the magnifier to determine the results of the test.

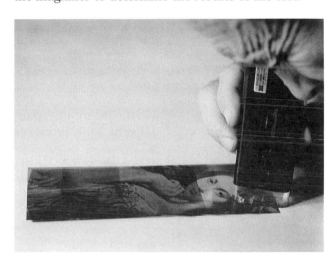

8. **Below:** In determining the results of the main exposure look at the test segment that will give a partially formed dot or immature dot in the whitest areas of the image.

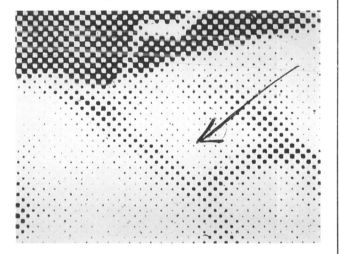

If this dot is too well formed in all of the test segments, decrease the exposure time for each segment and retest. If there is absolutely no dot, then the time increments should be increased.

In high contrast negatives, the immature dot may never appear and if it does, it may cause the other dots to 'fill in'.

There are some circumstances where the immature dot will not appear. Chief consideration should be given to the **structure of the remaining dots** to make sure none of them have filled in. If there are no whites in the original negative there should be no immature dots either, just small solid dots. This will depend on the grey tone the dots are representing.

9. Once the best exposure has been determined, test again with a fresh piece of lith film before carrying out the **shadow detail exposure**.

Below: The testing procedure is followed as before, but this time the lith film should ideally cross from the whitest to the darkest areas. In the example below the best place to position the test strip is across the face of the figure in the foreground.

The film is taped down at one edge and the contact screen placed on top.

If the first main exposure test determined the optimum exposure to be, say, 6 seconds, then at this point the second piece of film is given a 6 second exposure. After this exposure the vacuum is shut off and the contact screen is carefully removed (this is why the film is taped down, as removing the screen may move the film) then the glass lid is repositioned over the film and the vacuum turned on.

The piece of lith film that has already had a main exposure must be re-exposed without the contact screen on top, to determine the optimum **shadow detail exposure.**

Again, this test film is roughly divided into thirds and given three test exposures. A good ballpark figure to start with for a time increment is approximately one third of the time given to the main exposure. In this case, start with increments of 2 seconds.

Below: The test film will now have had three shadow detail test exposures of 2, 4, and 6 seconds respectively. After these exposures, the film is developed with agitation for 1.5 minutes, and without agitation for 1.5 minutes, then placed into the stop bath, fix and water bath as before.

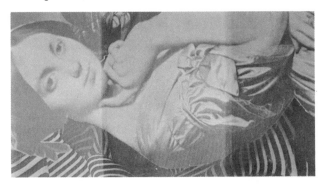

It is at this point that the shadow detail dot is examined under the magnifier.

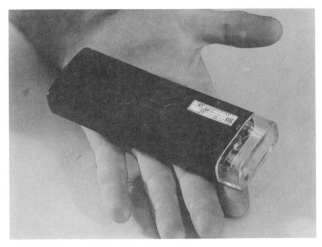

Above: The Radio Shack 30 x power pocket microscope.

Below: The main aspect to examine is the structure of the dots in the darkest areas. These dots must not be filled in; there should be some transparent areas between the dots. The amount of transparent area determines the black dot coverage which is ideal anywhere between 70% to 90%.

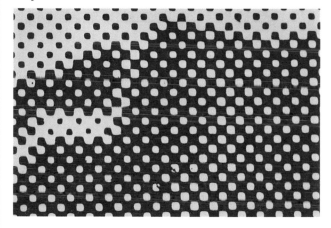

The black dot coverage will depend on the intensity of the blacks in the negative. Dark greys will be at the 70% end, and the pitch blacks will be at the 90% end. If the dots have filled in on the minimum exposure, then repeat the above test and decrease the time increments. If the dot structure is too open on the maximum test increment, then repeat the above test and increase the time increments until the optimum dot structure is achieved.

10. Once the optimum **main exposure** and **shadow detail exposure** have been determined, the lith film positive is ready to be made to the image size. The steps to do this are summarized as follows:

First: **main exposure** with screen.

Second: **shadow detail exposure** without screen.

Third: develop for 3 minutes, agitating for half that time and the remaining time without agitation.

Fourth: place in stop bath for 30 seconds.

Fifth: place into fixer bath until the lighter areas are completely transparent or for about 4 minutes.

Sixth: wash thoroughly in running water for about 10 minutes.

Seventh: hang to dry.

This may, at first, seem like a rather fastidious way to approach making a halftone, but it is, in fact, one of the easier methods. If making full tonal photo etchings is desired, this method will prove invaluable.

Above: Example of a dot structure that has filled in.

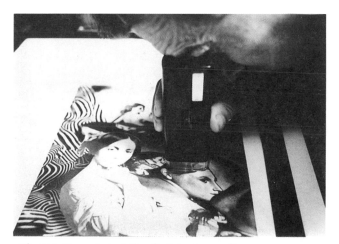

Above: Examining the finished results.

Alternate Lith Film Processes

Line Shot or Tone Drop-out

If a normal full tonal black and white photograph has all the intermittent tones between the black and white removed, the results would be a high contrast photograph.

One method of achieving this result is to enlarge a black and white negative directly onto lith film without using the halftone screen. Photographs translated into this form, can then become photo etchings through use of the "Howard Process", to achieve a unique creative effect. Commonplace photographs can be injected with a graphic quality that may have greater visual impact. It is important to realize that any photo etching, whether it be done with the halftone method or the tone drop-out method, can be creatively manipulated by various traditional methods. To limit the "Howard Process" to that of simply another method of photo reproduction is to severely limit the creative potential of this process.

Above: Full tone photograph.

How to Make a Tone Drop-out

This process is similar to the process of making a halftone, but does not employ the use of the halftone screen.

1. Place the negative into the enlarger and project image onto baseboard to focus and size up. Place tape onto the baseboard to mark the outside edge of the enlarged image.

2. Although there is a large exposure latitude with this method, it is still advisable to do a test strip. Place a strip of lith film, approximately 6" x 6", onto the baseboard so that it crosses between a black and white part of the image.

3. Set the enlarger aperture to F8. There are many variables in determining exposure (see pages 10 and 12.)

For the sake of explanation, I will be using time increments of 3 seconds. Have a covering card larger than the test strip in one hand, and expose the entire test film for 3 seconds. Cover about one third of the area of the test film with the card and expose it for another 3 seconds. Repeat this process by covering two thirds and exposing for an additional 3 seconds. This test strip has now had three separate exposures of 3, 6, and 9 seconds.

4. Develop, **with agitation** for 3 minutes.

The temperature of the developer is important. Make sure that it is between 68°F and 70°F. Try and keep all your liquids at the same temperature.

5. Place into stop bath for about 30 seconds.

6. Place into fixer until the lighter areas turn transparent.

7. Wash in running water.

The tone drop-out method will yield acceptable results but a lot of the middle tone grey detail may be lost. There is a method which can improve on the overall detail but employs one extra step. This step is called **flashing,** and is done after the optimum first exposure is determined.

Flashing is achieved by exposing the lith film to a naked blast of light. A preferred method is to take the negative out of the negative carrier of the enlarger, then return the empty negative carrier, stop down the enlarger lens to F22 or the smallest aperture possible, and expose the lith film with the white enlarger light source. Determining how much light to use is open to many variables, but generally this exposure has a latitude of .3 of a second to 1.5 of a second. Again, a test strip will determine the optimum exposure for the particular negative being used. Observation of the test results will be the determining factor and in some cases the result may exceed the exposure latitudes given.

When the flashing technique is used it is important to remove the negative from the enlarger and stop the aperture down to the smallest f stop.

Bas-relief

Bas-relief is a commonly known photographic technique used to enhance the graphic possibilities of a photograph. This process works best with images that have a high degree of detail and are also high in contrast.

Bas-relief basically involves making a positive tone drop-out and a negative tone drop-out, sandwiching them together, slightly out of register, then contact exposing this composite to a piece of lith film of equal size.

Above: A positive and negative tone drop-out by Ken Burkholder. The bas-relief image made from the above can be seen on the following page.

Above: The positive on the left was made with a single 3 second exposure directly onto the lith film. The same image on the right had an additional 0.3 of a second flash exposure. The flash exposure brings out more detail.

Making a Bas-relief

1. Make a positive tone drop-out as described previously (page 15).

2. Take the negative out of the enlarger, returning the negative carrier.

3. In the vacuum frame, place the positive tone drop-out onto an unexposed piece of lith film. Close the glass frame, ensuring that the positive tone drop-out is firmly contacted onto the lith film.

4. The lith film is then exposed to a short blast of direct light from the enlarger. As the positive tone drop-out is an opaque black, the exposure latitude here is very large. The problem is not to underexpose the lith film. Make a test strip by giving a piece of lith film a 5 second blast of light with the aperture open to F4.

5. Develop, stop, fix and wash as described in making the tone drop-out on page 15.

6. Up to this point, a tone drop-out lith film positive and negative have been made. Positive and negative are sandwiched together, slightly off-setting them, the amount of offset will create a graphic delineation of the original photograph.

The result is "contact printed" onto another piece of lith film in the same manner in which the negative tone drop-out was made, resulting in a positive linear representation similar to an outline drawing.

New Method of Developing Tri-X, Recording Film and High Speed Infrared Film for Unique Grain

Of particular interest to photographers is a completely new method of developing the above 35mm films that gives a unique grain structure to the finished print. The secret to this new method is to develop the film in Kodak's Super RT developer. This developer is made up from a **powdered concentrate** and comes as a part A and part B developer. The developer is made up by adding 1 part of A to 6 parts of water then adding one part of B.

Development is carried out between 68°F-70°F. The method of development is the same for conventional black and white films. When using Tri-X, rate the film at 400 ASA and develop in the Super RT developer for 15 minutes.

Ratc Kodak's Recording film 2475 at 1600 ASA and develop in the Super RT developer for 10 minutes at 68°F.

Kodak's High Speed Infrared Film is rated at 400 ASA (use no filter and expose to two 500 watt tungsten lights) and developed in Super RT developer for 15 minutes at 68°F.

If you wish to make lith film positives using the Super RT Developer method the best results occur from negatives that appear to be under exposed. To achieve this, re-rate each film and develop as follows:

1. Tri-X, rated at 1600 ASA, developed for 15 minutes at 70°F.
2. Recording film rated at 1600 ASA, developed for 5 minutes at 70°F.
3. High Speed Infrared film rated at 1600 ASA, developed for 15 minutes at 68°F.

These negatives can be directly enlarged onto lith film resulting in a random mezzotint type dot structure. Use the 'flashing' technique, previously mentioned on page 16, to obtain the best results.

Above: Bas-relief etching by Ken Burkholder.

Above: This photograph was used by photographer John Stewart to produce the unique photo etched image below.

Above: Etching utilizing the "Howard Process" by John Stewart. John used a tone drop-out with sprayed aquatint for this print.

Handmade and Photocopy Stencils

The halftone positive and the tone drop-out are examples of stencils generated solely within the darkroom. As the acetate sheet is the vehicle for the photo emulsion, almost anything else that has similar transparency can act as the vehicle and any opaque substance can replace the photo emulsion.

Architects' tracing paper (drafting film) makes an ideal substitute for the acetate and any opaque ink or poster paint will replace the photo emulsion. Herculene Drafting film .003 thick with a matt 2 finish is a commonly available drafting film in Canada. It comes in sheets or rolls and makes an ideal vehicle for carrying ink or drawn marks. There are clear polyester and acetate sheets also available that will work equally as well.

Below: A variety of interesting textures can be transferred to the tracing paper by placing it onto a textured surface and rubbing the top matt surface with a 3B pencil.

The textured drafting film with penciled on texture can then be exposed to the dried, gelatin-coated plate, developed and etched. The plate may need to be aquatinted before being etched (see page 71).

See the section on using the New Soft-Ground Method for further types of stencil carrying papers (see pages 73-77).

The Direct "Positive" Method

Another method is to draw and paint directly onto the dried photo-sensitive gelatin emulsion of the etching plate. The best type of ink to use for this purpose is Pelican's Water Soluble India Ink *made for fountain pens*. Another substitute that can be used is a paint made by Kodak called Kodak Opaque. This is earth red coloured pigment, made from jeweler's rouge, is completely opaque and washes away easily in water. It is important to use inks or paints that are both **opaque** and **water soluble**. The technique of the direct positive method is as follows:

1. **Below:** Under subdued light draw or paint directly onto the sensitized gelatin coated plate with Pelican's India Ink.

2. The exposure can be done by placing the plate into direct sunlight for about 5 minutes. This time may vary according to the type of day and to the time of day the exposure is made. In the beginning make a test plate, with whatever exposure source you have elected to use, to determine the correct exposure.

3. **Below:** After the plate is exposed to a UV light source it is washed in hot water (110°F to 120°F) using a gentle circular motion with cotton balls.

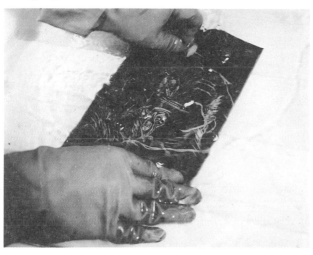

4. The plate may need to be aquatinted before being etched (see section 'Aquatinting' page 71).

5. The back of the plate is sealed, then etched (see page 58) and printed (see pages 63-66).

Above: The plate after being developed in hot water.

The Photocopy Stencil

Any image that can be photocopied can be utilized in some way by the "Howard Process". The quality of the finished etched image will depend on the type of photo that is photocopied and whether this copied image is made on paper or acetate.

It is not widely known, but most copiers copy onto acetate just as well as they do onto paper. These copies make the best stencils. If acetate cannot be used, any normal one-sided photocopy can be substituted, provided vegetable oil is wiped over the entire surface of the photocopy prior to exposing it to the plate. This makes the photocopy paper more translucent.

In both the handmade and photocopy stencils it may be necessary to add an aquatint before etching the plate (see pages 71-72).

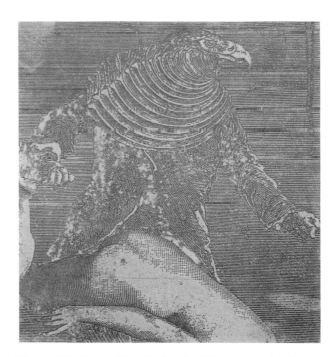

Above: Etching, 5" x 5", by Jo Wilson, made during the "Howard Process" workshop held at the Australian Print Workshop, Melbourne, Australia.

The Direct "Negative" Method

The Direct "Negative" Method

This is a method that requires the direct block-out application of Hunt Speedball's screen filler Number 4570 or 4530 to a degreased aquatinted plate. The plate can be progressively blocked out and etched between each blocking-out procedure or it can be blocked-out only once. If the plate is only blocked-out once the resulting line will be white and the surrounding area will be any tone from grey to black depending on how long the plate is etched.

1. **Below:** Painting the Hunt Speedball screen filler onto a previously aquatinted plate.

2. **Below:** Progressively blocking-out the plate with brush and screen filler.

After the plate has been etched the screen filler is removed with a fifty percent dilution of household bleach and water. Spray household cleaners such as Mr. Clean or Wisk will also remove the screen filler.

To fully understand how to utilize these types of stencils, a greater understanding of the actual photo etching process, as described on page 49, is recommended. However, once the etching process is understood, the combination of these techniques with others outlined in this book should open up new avenues of creative possibilities.

3. **Below:** Progressively blocking-out the plate.

4. **Below:** Because the plate was progressively blocked-out and etched, several tones were made resulting in the following print.

Above: An example of how flexible the "Howard Process" is can be demonstrated with the above plate. This plate was etched to the point that three holes were etched through the plate. The resulting print from this plate can be seen on page 48.

The Stock Sensitizing Solution

The sensitizing solution is prepared by mixing either potassium dichromate or ammonium dichromate crystals with distilled water.

Potassium dichromate is slightly less sensitive to light and cheaper than ammonium dichromate. Both can be used in a dimly lit studio, for short periods of time, without fear of exposing the plate.

The stock sensitizing solution can be made up in **three different strengths** to accommodate your method of exposure and studio conditions.

Preparing the Stock Sensitizing Solution

Material list:
1. Potassium Dichromate or Ammonium Dichromate.

2. Gram or ounce scale.

3. One litre **(1 quart)** of distilled water**.

4. One litre **(1 quart)** measuring container.

5. Amber storage bottle or light-proof container to store one litre **(1 quart)** of liquid or more. Any container can be made light-proof by spraying the outside with black spray paint or by sticking red Mac Tac (brand name for a self adhesive plastic sometimes used to cover books or shelves) on the outside.

6. Rubber gloves, dust mask, and work apron.

Health and Safety Procedure

This part of the "Howard Process" is considered the most hazardous, but if rubber gloves, eye protection, and respirator with HEPA cartridges are worn, when preparing this solution, they should provide adequate safety protection.

Dichromates are very poisonous in the pure granular form but when dissolved in water the toxicity is reduced considerably. (Potassium and ammonium dichromate have such a high boiling point that they do not evaporate into the air at the temperatures used in the "Howard Process".) When this stock sensitizing solution is used in the final gelatin solution, it is diluted with more water, further reducing its toxicity (see page 88).

Mixing Procedure

1. **Mild Sensitizer:** Measure 30 grams **(1 oz.)** of potassium dichromate and add to one litre **(1 quart)** of distilled water. This was the strength of sensitizer used in the gelatin emulsion tested in the health and safety report on page 88. (Please read this report before continuing.) This strength sensitizer is best suited to open studios where it is difficult to control stray light and is best used with a high powered UV light source for exposing the emulsion.

2. **Medium sensitizer:** Measure 60 grams **(2 oz.)** of potassium dichromate and add to one litre **(1 quart)** of distilled water. This strength sensitizer will effectively reduce exposure time by about 20% from that of the mild sensitizer and is best used in a studio with low lighting.

3. **Strong sensitizer:** Measure 90 grams **(3 oz.)** of potassium dichromate and add to one litre **(1 quart)** of distilled water. This strength sensitizer will reduce exposure time by 40% to 50% from that of the mild sensitizer and is best used in a dimly lit studio.

Remember that ammonium dichromate can be substituted for potasium dichromate.

The sensitizer solution should be mixed thoroughly and let stand, in a dark cupboard for one day, before adding to the gelatin.

This 1 litre batch **(1 quart)** of sensitizing solution, when added to the gelatin, will make 10 litres **(2.19 gal.)** of gelatin solution.

If a gram or ounce scale is not readily available, **a simple method of measuring 30 grams (1 oz.)** is to make a balance scale with a 12" wooden ruler by balancing it on the square side of a pencil. Place the ruler on top of the pencil, at the 6" middle section, so that both ends of the ruler are equally balanced. Take a small quantity of sand and a styrofoam cup to your local pharmacy or high school science teacher and ask them to measure exactly 30 grams **(1 oz.)**. This will be your counter balance. Now place this at one end of the ruler and an empty styrofoam cup at the other and add the sensitizer crystals to the empty cup until the balance is equalized.

** 1 litre = approx. 34 oz.   1 US quart = 32 oz.
7 grams = 1/4 oz. (0.25 oz)

Biagio Maiorino, photo etching, "Adam and Eve", 6" x 9". This etching made from a collage of old engravings utilizing the "Howard Process". The collage was photocopied onto acetate and printed in intaglio and relief.

Making the Double Boiler

Knox Gelatine is made up with hot distilled water, and when this mixture reaches room temperature the gelatin solidifies. To successfully use the "Howard Process", a double boiler will have to be made before mixing up your first batch of gelatin. A double boiler in this instance is made up of a small container submerged in water inside a larger container. The water inside the larger container is kept at a constant temperature between 110° and 120°F with an aquarium heater.

Fast food shops, bakeries, and restaurants generally have a great variety of containers that are regularly discarded, and it is these containers that can be used to make the double boiler. Inexpensive plastic containers that will equally serve the purpose can be purchased at the local hardware store (see page 97).

The first double boiler illustrated is made from a 3 gallon ice cream bucket which has a lid that can easily be removed. The inside container is a 4 litre (1 gal.) plastic container purchased at the local hardware store.

The second double boiler is made from a 16 litre (4.2 gal.) bulk cooking oil container with an internal container made from a 4 litre (1 gal.) batter mix container. The batter mix container was obtained at the local bakery.

To convert these two containers into double boilers the **following materials** will be needed:

1. 8" Radiant aquarium heater purchased at the local pet store. If this heater is not available, look at the illustration and try and match it as closely as possible.

2. 2" x 14" of half-inch Poly "B" tubing, available at your local plumbing supply store.

3. Sharp knife.

4. Half inch drill bit and drill.

5. Sill Plate Gasket or foam rubber ironing board cover. This can be taped onto the outside of the double boilers, with ducting tape, to insulate it.

The Ice Cream Bucket Conversion

1. **Below:** An opening 1 1/2" x 1 1/2" is cut about 2" down from the top lip of the container. This opening will house the aquarium heater.

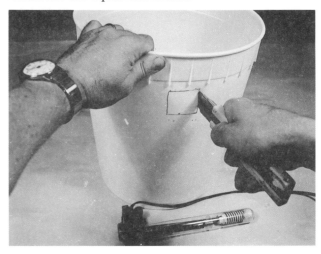

2. **Below:** Drill one 5/8" hole 7 1/2" up from the bottom of the container on opposing sides of the container to accommodate the 1/2" wide Poly "B" tubing.

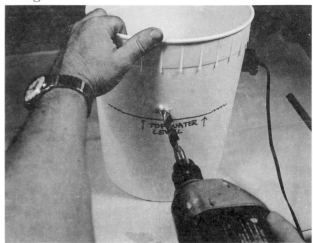

3. **Below:** To set the temperature of the aquarium heater, take the temperature control knob off the top of the heater, and screw the flange that the knob was attached to, clockwise until it stops. Before replacing this knob, smear vaseline over the flange, particularly where the flange comes out of the heater housing, to make it completely waterproof. (This part of the heater does have water fall onto it due to the condensation inside the double boiler.)

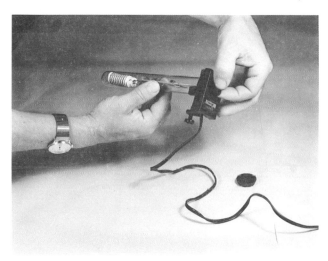

4. **Below:** The aquarium heater is now ready to be installed and is best done from the inside of the container by first feeding the electrical cord out through the hole .

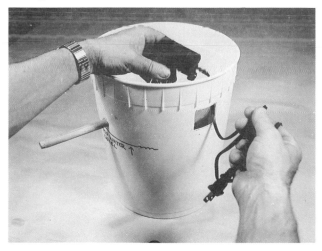

In unheated studios, purchase some type of flexible insulation material to wrap around the double boiler to keep the heat in. Sill Plate Gasket, purchased from the local building supply store, or an ironing board foam padding are ideal.

5. **Below:** It is a good idea at this point to mark the water level on the outside of the container. Mark the water level when the gelatin container is out of the large container and again when it is inside. This is easily done by filling the gelatin container almost completely up with water and dropping it into the larger container. The water level, in both instances, can be seen on the outside of the container and marked.

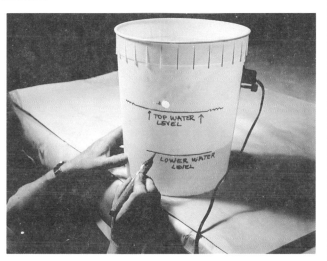

6. Place the Poly "B" tubing through the access holes at the top and fill the container until the water level indicated on the aquarium heater is reached. Mark this top water line, then remove the inside gelatin container and mark the lower water level. When it is necessary to add water, this can be done with the gelatin container inside or outside of the larger container. When water is first added, it should be hot and any water added later should also be hot. If cold water is added it may crack the glass tube of the aquarium heater.

Another very important point is to **unplug the aquarium heater before taking the internal gelatin holding container out.** If the heater is left on, after the internal container is removed, the water level will drop below its proper level. Subsequently, when the gelatin container is replaced, the water level rises rapidly around a hot aquarium heater and cracks the glass. If this heater glass is broken, replacement tubes can be ordered from the original store the heater was purchased from.

The Cooking Oil Container Conversion

Below: Another alternative to making the double boiler is to use a 16 litre **(4.2 gal.)** all-purpose cooking oil container and a 4 litre **(1 gal.)** batter mix container. Most restaurants use and discard these types of containers.

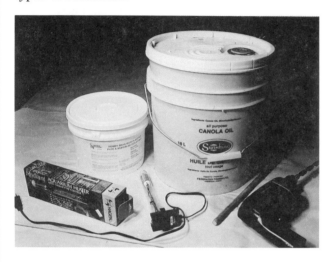

Below: When converting the 16 litre **(4.2 gal.)** cooking oil container, cut the lip off the lid otherwise the lid is almost impossible to open.

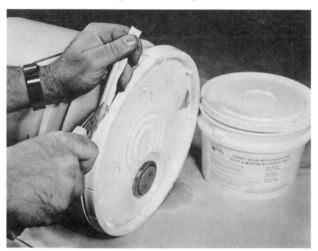

It is very important not to leave the double boiler heater pluged in and unattended for more than a couple of days as the water level will eventually drop, through evaporation, which may result in the heater burning a hole through the double bolier.

Below: The design of this double boiler is very similar to the first except an extra stabilizing 1/2" Poly "B" tube (available at most plumbing supply stores) is needed because this container is wider than the previous one. Drill two 5/8" holes, directly above the lower lip, to accommodate the Poly "B" tubing.

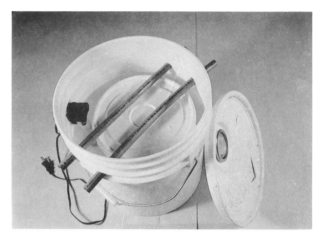

It is possible to use other combinations of containers. The main consideration is that the aquarium heater has sufficient clearance to hang freely inside the larger container and that the smaller inside gelatin holding container floats (submerged up to a level just below the lid) in water heated by the aquarium heater. A lid on the larger container is advisable as it reduces evaporation of the hot water.

Below: Any external holes should be taped up to further reduce evaporation of the water inside the double boiler.

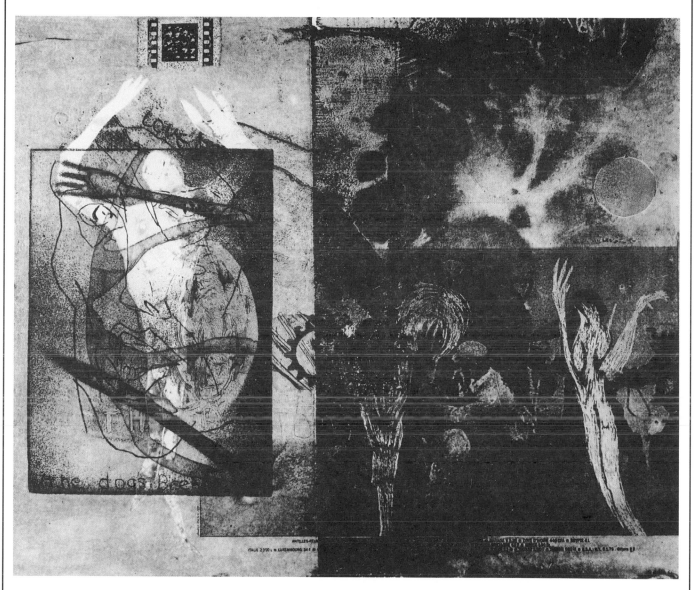

Victoria Edgar, photo etching, utilizing the "Howard Process", with hand drawn stencils and aquatint, 11" x 14".

Preparing the Gelatin Emulsion

In preparing 1 litre **(1 US quart)** of gelatin emulsion the following materials will be required:

1. Two 84 gram boxes of Knox Unflavoured Gelatine as packaged in Canada or one **8 oz. box** of Knox Unflavoured Gelatine as packaged in the U.S.A.

2. 200 ml **(7 oz.)** of potassium or ammonium dichromate sensitizing solution (see page 88).

3. 200 ml **(7 oz.)** of cold distilled water.

4. 400 ml **(14 oz.)** of boiling distilled water.

5. One 55 ml **(2 oz.)** bottle of Food Club blue food colouring.**

6. One litre **(1 US quart)** measuring container.

7. An electric kettle to boil the distilled water.

8. A double boiler (see page 25).

9. One stirring stick or spoon.

Mixing 1 litre or 1 quart of Gelatin Solution

1. Below: First step. Using the inside container from the double boiler as the mixing vessel, add 200 ml **(7 oz.)** of cold <u>distilled water</u>.

Remember that the stock sensitizing solution can be made up in three different strengths (see page 23).

2. Below: Second step. Add 200 ml **(7 oz.)** of dichromate sensitizing solution.

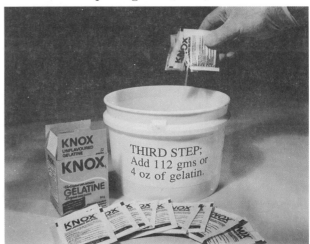

3. Below: Third step. Sprinkle 112 grams **(8 oz.)** of Knox Gelatine granules onto the sensitizing solution and stir slowly for 1 minute. (16 seven gram packets or 16 **1/4 oz (.25 oz.)** packets of Knox Gelatine make up 112 grams **(8 oz.).**

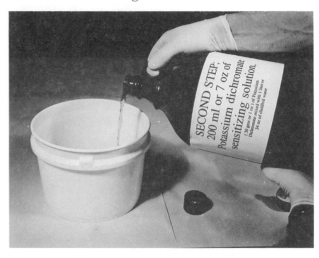

**The colour blue is used because the plate is exposed to an ultraviolet light source which is also blue in colour. If red or yellow colouring is used it may inhibit the exposure of the gelatin (see pages 97 and 98 for sources of supply and alternate colourings).

4. **Below: Forth step.** To this add one 55 ml **(2 oz.)** container of blue Food Club food colouring. Food Club is a brand name of food colouring available in Canada and can be purchased in bulk quantities. This colouring is added so that the final exposed image is visible on the plate. Some **brands of food colouring, that I have tried, have not worked successfully because of the addition of a dispersant. This dispersant breaks down the surface tension of the gelatin emulsion making it impossible to achieve an even coating. Water Soluble India Ink makes a good substitute.**

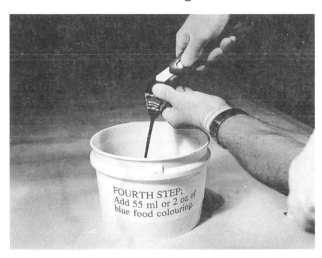

5. **Below: Fifth Step.** Then add 400 ml **(14 oz.)** of boiling distilled water.

A thinner solution (good for fine detail) can be made by adding an *additional* 200 ml. **(7 oz.)** of boiling distilled water at the above **Fifth Step.**

6. Slowly stir the gelatin mixture.

7. Place lid onto gelatin container and put container into the double boiler.

It is a good practice to clean the gelatin holding container thoroughly each time it is used.

Any larger or smaller batches of gelatin can be made up. If, for instance, half of the above quantity is required, divide all the ingredients by 50% and if double the above quantity is required double the quantity of each ingredient.

When this solution is first made up it is almost impossible to use for the dip coating method because of the bubbles created during mixing. If this solution is mixed carefully and slowly, it should be ready to use within the hour. Again, it is advisable to have a double boiler to keep this solution soluble.

Once the original gelatin solution is depleted, more solution can be added by making up another batch. If this solution is kept under constant heat in the double boiler, it has a life of about 5 weeks. The 'shelf life' of the heated gelatin solution will depend on the extent with which the dichromate sensitizer has oxidized.

It is also important to note that if this gelatin emulsion is left in a double boiler, that has a water temperature **exceeding** 120°F, the gelatin will solidify through cooking.

It is possible to allow the gelatin to solidify and to return it to the double boiler to redissolve. (Provided it has not cooked.) This will take about 5 hours. This is not a good practice as there are sometimes particles that do not redissolve and if these undissolved particles get into the liquid emulsion during the plate coating process, problems may result.

It may be necessary to use only **distilled water** when making up the stock sensitizing solution and the gelatin emulsion. The phosphates and minerals in tap water can create 'free acids' when the plate is etched in the ferric chloride solution. This causes certain areas of the gelatin to break down during etching, resulting in "black pitting" of the final print. Try your local tap water first to see if this pitting occurs.

Preparing the Copper Plate

What Type of Copper to Buy

The most economical type of copper to buy for the etching processes outlined in this book is roofing copper, the type used by plumbers and roofing contractors.

Below: Roofing copper is sold by its thickness and its weight. The one that is the most economical and flexible is referred to as 16 oz. copper sheet. This copper is 0.022" thick and heavy enough to permit a deep bite and to use both sides of the plate. 16 oz. copper comes in 8' x 3' sheets. Generally, the companies that sell this copper will cut it into whatever size is required (see page 98).

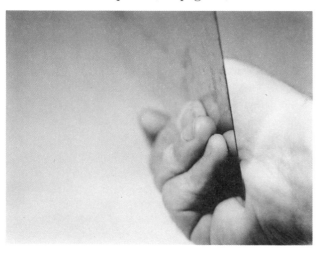

Currently, copper is about half the cost of unsensitized zinc plates, and about one quarter the cost of pre-sensitized zinc plates or engraver's copper.

This inexpensive roofing copper has one drawback. It may come with very fine surface scratches, which can easily be removed with 320 grit wet-and-dry sandpaper.

Printmakers often ask the question, "why not use zinc for the "Howard Process"?" Zinc is an inferior metal for etching. Being more expensive and softer than copper, it loses its printing definition faster, and also has a host of other problems related to the nitric acid solution that most printmakers use to etch the plate. Using zinc has only been a recent phenomenon in etching. Copper and steel have been the preferred metal for hundreds of years.

Materials Needed for Preparing the Plate

1. 320 grit wet-and-dry sandpaper.

2. Electric sander.

3. Comet cleanser, (a white powdered household cleanser that contains a mild abrasive and degreasing agent commonly used to clean pots and pans).

4. Pots and pans scrubber pad.

5. Rubber dishwashing gloves.

6. Sink with running water.

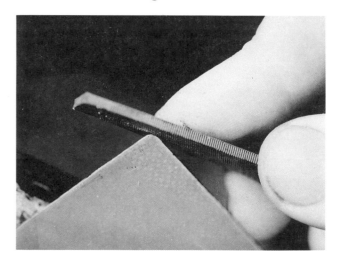

Above: It is a good practice to round off the metal corners of the etching plate with a small file as there is less likelihood of these corners snagging the tarlatan during the wiping and printing process outlined on pages 63 to 66.

The price of copper sheeting varies considerably from one supplier to the next and can be purchased in a variety of thicknesses. A price comparison check is prudent. Also, check to see if these suppliers sell smaller off-cuts of copper and if they will cut down a larger sheet and how much their cutting fee is.

Plate Preparation

1. **Below:** Prepare one side of the plate by first sanding with the 320 grit wet-and-dry sandpaper (use with water). This sanding should be sufficient to remove all the fine surface scratches and to give the plate a perfect tooth for the emulsion to adhere to.

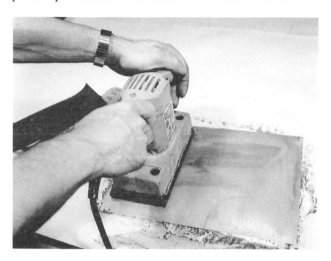

If deep scratches remain, scrape and burnish to remove (see page 83).

2. **Below:** Scratch being removed with burnisher. Use the smooth surface of the burnisher. Always put a small amount of lightweight oil onto the area to be burnished. Hold the burnisher with one hand and apply pressure with the other.

3. **Below:** After sanding, rinse the residue off with water. Put on the rubber gloves, sprinkle the Comet powder onto the plate and scrub it vigorously with a plastic pots and pans scrubber. This is a very important step, as this is what degreases the plate. The rubber gloves prevent greasy finger prints from being deposited onto the plate.

It is possible to completely by-pass preparing the copper plate with the aid of the electric sander by scrubbing the plate with Comet cleanser and a stainless steel curled wire type of pot scrubber.

4. **Below:** After the plate has been thoroughly degreased rinse with hot running water, then squeegee off the excess water with a photo print squeegee or blot off this excess water with paper towels.

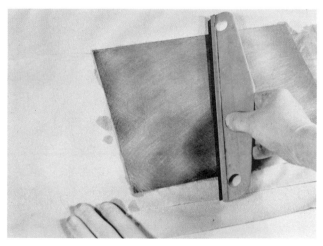

Applying the Gelatin Emulsion

Dip Coating the Copper Plate

This method involves dipping a prepared copper plate twice into the liquid gelatin. The **first** coat is dipped and dried rapidly in front of a fan and left for at least two hours to dry completely. The plate is propped up vertically to dry and, since the gelatin dries as it falls, the plate dries with an uneven coat of gelatin. To compensate for this uneven first coating a **second** coat is applied, drying the plate upside down to the first coat. The plate is then left in a darkened cupboard until it is ready to use.

Best results are achieved when the sensitized gelatin coated plates are used within the first few days. The dichromate sensitizers are subject to a gradual darkening, **even if stored in a dark place.** This darkening occurs to the emulsion as soon as one week or as long as 6 weeks after the plate has been coated and is known as the 'dark reaction'. This 'dark reaction' is similar to exposing the plate to direct light and effectively desensitizes the gelatin emulsion. If this occurs the plate must be completely cleaned and recoated.

Necessary Materials for Dip Coating

1. Photo developing tray for the gelatin emulsion that will accommodate the size of the etching plate to be coated.

2. Darkroom thermometer.

3. A larger tray than the tray holding the gelatin emulsion.

4. Unprinted newsprint paper.

5. Surgical gloves.

6. Eye protection.

7. Work apron.

8. Electric fan.

9. Light-proof storage cupboard.

Dip Coating Procedure

This coating procedure should be carried out in subdued light.

Wear your apron and surgical gloves for this procedure.

1. **Below:** Set up your working area so that everything is easily accessible.

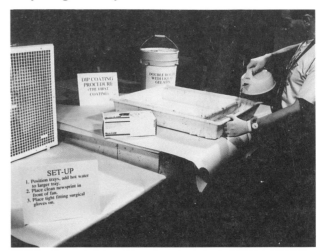

2. Unplug the double boiler which is holding the gelatin and plug in the fan.

3. **Below:** Carefully pour the gelatin emulsion into the smaller photo tray. Do this slowly to prevent bubbles forming .

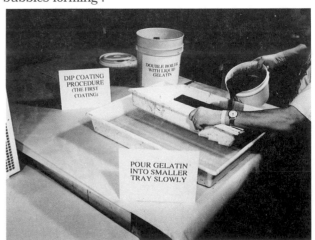

4A. Below: Slowly lower the prepared copper plate into the gelatin.

4B.

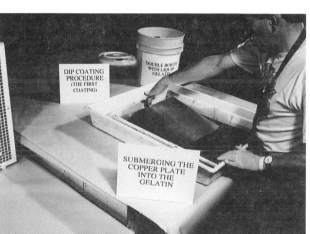

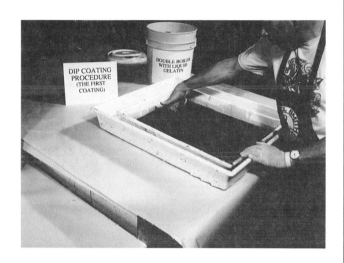

5A. Below: Photo trays are manufactured with a groove in the bottom. Run a gloved finger down this groove to come up from under the submerged plate and prop it vertically in the tray. Examine the surface of the plate for air bubbles or other imperfections. If air bubbles are present, wipe to one side with a thumb and repeat the dip coating procedure until there are no bubbles.

5B.

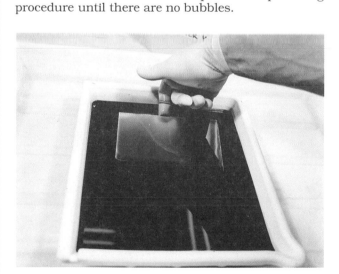

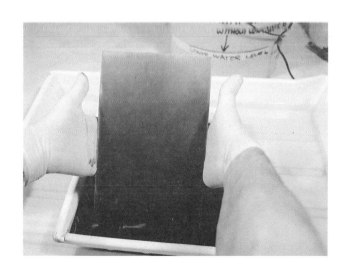

6. **Below:** When the plate is free of blemishes, open the palms of your hands to make the surgical gloves as taut as possible, then clasp the plate between your palms being careful not to disturb the downward runoff of the gelatin. Any disturbance of the natural downward flow of the gelatin will cause an irregularity in the even distribution of the gelatin.

Air bubbles floating on the surface of the gelatin emulsion can interrupt the even coating of the plate. One method to avoid these bubbles, (requiring a little practice) is to rock the tray, containing the gelatin, to and fro. The bubbles will travel from one side of the tray to the other. It is a matter of timing to trap the bubbles at one end of the tray while raising the copper plate out of the gelatin at the other end.

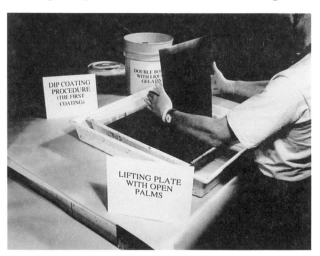

7A. **Below:** Lift the plate from the gelatin tray and prop up vertically in front of the fan.

7B.

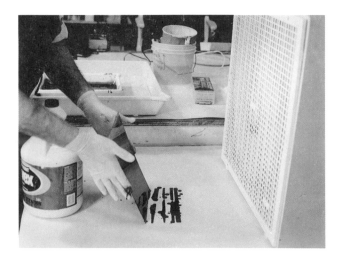

8A. Below: Wait a few seconds and slowly 'walk' the plate backwards, allowing the run-off residue to fall onto the paper. Do this until the run-off stops, then prop the plate up vertically to dry in a darkened cupboard.

8B. NB. When holding the gelatin coated plate make sure that the finger tips are pointed towards each other in such a way that the hands form the vertical sides of a triangle.

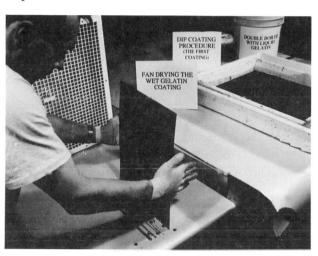

Above: Etching, 6" x 4 1/2", by the author utilizing the dip-coating method. The above image was made from an 85 line halftone screen and was etched for 3 hours in 42 Baume ferric chloride solution. This was the first print pulled.

Applying the Gelatin Emulsion: Continued

Due to the blue colouring, the plate will show a perfect gradation from light blue to darker blue. This results from the natural vertical fall of the gelatin while solidifying onto the surface of the plate. There is a thinner deposit of gelatin on the top of the plate that gradually gets thicker towards the bottom. To even out this coating it is necessary to recoat the plate, in the same manner as the first coat, by reversing the vertical flow of gelatin. Just prop the plate upside down.

It is important to let the first coat dry completely before attempting the second coat.

Do not touch the gelatin coating with an ungloved hand as this will disturb it, leaving a deposit of oil from the skin that will inhibit the application of the second coat and the ultimate etching process.

If the wet gelatin coated plate is left in front of a fan (in subdued light) the first coat should be dry within the hour. If the gelatin on the back of the plate is dry to the touch then the gelatin on the front should also be dry. Since the emulsion dulls as it dries it is possible to determine whether the emulsion is dry by examining the plate at an acute angle to the light.

Speed drying of the wet gelatin is possible by submerging the wet gelatin plate in a bath of rubbing alcohol prior to propping it vertically in front of the fan. The alcohol bath draws the water out of the gelatin and promotes speedy drying. Plates prepared in this manner do not perform as well as plates that are allowed to dry naturally.

Below: The second coating is prepared as the first except that the vertical flow of the gelatin is reversed. Invariably with the second coating, there seems to be a stray bubble or two. The best way to remove these bubbles is to wipe them to one side with a gloved thumb and resubmerge the plate into the gelatin bath.

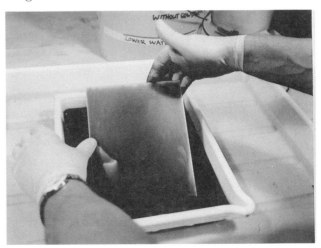

Make sure the temperature of the gelatin does not fall below 100° F. If this happens the gelatin coating will be deposited too thickly, which will result in some loss of detail in the finished print.

The number of plates that can be coated at one time will depend on how fast they can be prepared. It is possible to add a heater to the water-carrying tray and a plexiglass lid will keep the heat in for extended classroom use.

At first this dip coating method may seem to be rather difficult but with a little patience and practice perfectly coated plates will result.

Above: Skintight surgical gloves are recommended.

Alain Costaz, "War Dreams". This etching , 6" x 9", utilizes the "Howard Process" and was made from a photocopied collage. The image was spray aquatinted before etching and printed intaglio and relief. (See page 78.)

Victoria Edgar, "True Love ". Etching, 6" x 9", utilizing the "Howard Process". Made from a colour snapshot photocopied onto acetate with dot screen. The acetate was scratched to increase the tonal range. This plate was printed in combination with other plates and Chine Colled. (Chine Colled is a French word that, used in this context, means laminating under the pressure of the etching press, one paper into the surface of another in such a way that they appear to be one piece of paper.)

The Spray Coating Method

The Spray Coating Method

This at first may appear to be the simplest method of coating a plate. Although it is simple, it yields **vastly differing results** depending on the thickness of the spray. This technique has a uniqueness and integrity of its own. Rather than being a technique that produces a reproduction of a photograph, this is the **first** photo etching process that can abstract and creatively interpret photo reality.

Materials

1. Air brush. The Paasche air brush, single action model H, with the number 3 spray nozzle and the 3 oz. reservoir bottle is the type used in the accompanying illustrations.

2. Air compressor. Almost any air compressor will do the job. The Campbell Hansfeld Power Pal air compressor with a maximum PSI of 100 was used for the prints illustrated. Most air compressors will work with this technique.

3. Respirator with HEPA cartridges, eye protection, apron, and rubber gloves.

4. Spray booth. (This is not an absolute necessity as the spraying technique can be done anywhere if necessary.)

Health and Safety Precautions

The following method, **using the mild strength potassium dichromate solution**, was tested by the Alberta Government Occupational Health and Safety Department. A large copper plate was sprayed continuously for 2.5 hours and the overspray tested for toxicity. The test results showed the overspray to be approximately 55 times lower than minimum acceptable level of the Alberta occupational standards. Testing measured the amount of potassium dichromate in the sprayed gelatin mist for a radius of 10'. (The ammonium dichromate solution was not tested.)

Regardless of how safe this procedure is, the use of respirator, gloves, apron, and eye protection is still advised. **See further health and safety information on page 88.**

Spray Coating Procedure

1. Prepare and degrease copper plate in the manner described in 'Plate Preparation' on page 32.

2. **Below:** Tape a clean piece of newsprint, 12" larger than the dimensions of the plate, onto the wall behind the plate about to be sprayed.

3. Prop the prepared copper plate against the newsprint.

4. Fill the air brush reservoir with the gelatin emulsion, turn compressor on and test the quality of the spray using the newsprint. Most air brushes have an adjustable spray nozzle that will give a coarse or fine spray.

5. If fine detail is desired in the finished print, it will be necessary to apply as many as 50 very fine layers of gelatin emulsion. If a coarser spray with fewer layers is applied, the image becomes more diffused.

There are many different results that can be attained with this process according to the thickness and number of gelatin layers.

If overspray from the above method is a concern the **Dick Blick Art Materials** catalogue lists an excellent 'Airbrush Spray-Away Booth' (catalogue number 746800) which filters the spray through carbon filters and will quietly and efficiently eliminate airbrush overspray in your studio. Check the Dick Blick catalogue for more details. (See page 99)

When applying the spray coating, spray continuously and evenly from one side of the plate to the other. Always start spraying the air brush onto the backing paper, as the spray may give some unwanted splatters when it is first activated.

1. **Below**: Spray coating.

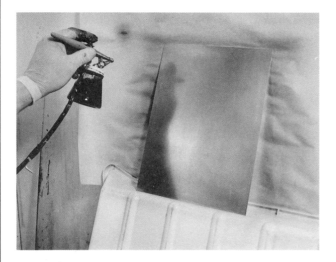

2. **Below**: Spray coating.

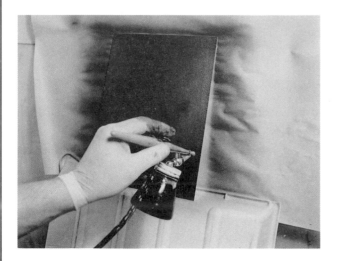

3. **Below**: Spray coating.

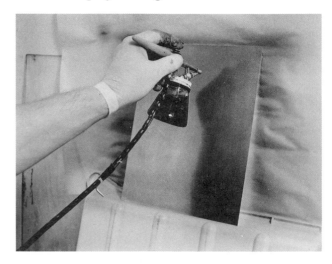

4. **Below**: Spray coating.

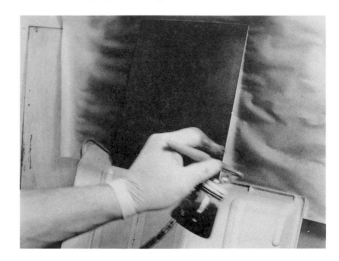

Try to lay down approximately 50 very fine coatings of gelatin. The first couple of layers should be fine and difficult to see, and eventually the coating will take on a colour similar to that of a dip coated plate.

Expose, develop, etch, and print this plate to evaluate the results. More or fewer layers may be required. This is a starting point for developing an understanding of the spraying technique. Experimenting further with thicker and fewer layers, varying the thickness and fineness of the spray from one part of the plate to the other will yield vastly different results.

Above: 3 X magnification of an exposed and developed plate that utilized the spray gelatin coating and an 85 line halftone image.

The Acetate Roll-up Variation

Another method that creates further interesting results is to interrupt the spray coating at any point and remove the partially sprayed plate to a table. Lay a clean stiff sheet of acetate onto the wet gelatin emulsion and roll on top of this acetate with a clean brayer or roller. The acetate is then removed, revealing a stippled surface that will change the nature of the finished print. Many further variations can be achieved by applying this roll-up technique at various stages while the gelatin is drying. The frequency and the degree of pressure on the roller will affect the eventual outcome of the print.

1. **Below:** Roll-up variation.

2. **Below:** Roll-up variation.

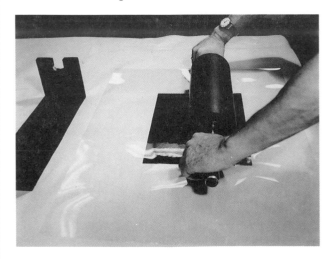

3. **Below:** Roll-up variation.

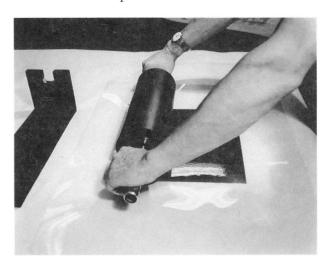

4. **Below:** Roll-up variation.

Joanne Kardaras, etching 6" x 5 1/2" made at the "Howard Process" workshop conducted at the Australian Print Workshop, Melbourne, Australia on June 28, 1991. This etching was made with the 'Hard Ground' method (page 73) that utilizes liquid floor finish as the ground.

Exposing and Developing the Plate

The Nature of the Exposing Process

Each lith film or hand made positive stencil is made up of **opaque** and **transparent** areas. The lith film or hand made positive is placed in contact with the sensitized gelatin emulsion and exposed to a strong blast of ultraviolet light. The opaque areas of the positive selectively prevent ultraviolet light from reaching the gelatin. These areas are unaffected by the light. The other areas harden due to the action of the ultraviolet light falling onto the surface.

Material Preparation

After the emulsion has dried, the plate is ready to be exposed to an ultraviolet light source.

There are **two methods** of exposing the plate. The **first** and preferred method, is with the aid of a vacuum frame or clamp down light box (see page 8). The **second** is the wet method and is done without the aid of a vacuum frame or light box.

The type of light source used to expose the plate can vary from direct sunlight to quartz halogen lights, to photography flood lights, to a mercury vapour light and finally to a tanning lamp. All these sources give off ultraviolet light and it is this type of light that is needed to selectively harden certain portions of the gelatin emulsion.

Other Materials

1. Photo tray, larger than the copper plate.

2. Large size cotton balls.

3. Rubber gloves.

4. Access to hot water.

5. 99% pure rubbing alcohol

6. Photographic print squeegee.

The Exposure

Exposure is governed by the strength of the light source, the distance that the light source is from the plate, the amount of sensitizer used in the gelatin emulsion and the length of the exposure.

Following are two examples which may prove to be a good starting point in determining exposure. Plates, dip coated with the mild potassium dichromate (see page 23) sensitized gelatin, that are exposed to direct sunlight with the **wet method** require an exposure of 5 to 10 minutes. (This is the exposure given to a normal 85 line halftone.) If a B.C.A No 1, 115-120V G.E Photo Flood light is placed about 12" from the vacuum frame an exposure of 6 minutes is required.

Whatever light source is used, it will be necessary to make a test exposure. Once the initial light strength of the exposure system being employed is known, further test exposures may not be necessary.

The length of light exposure to the sensitized gelatin plate will vary according to which sensitizer was used. The gelatin sensitized with potassium dichromate requires up to 15% more exposure time than plates sensitized with the ammonium dichromate solution.

To determine the optimum exposure with whatever method is employed, it will be necessary to make a step test exposure.

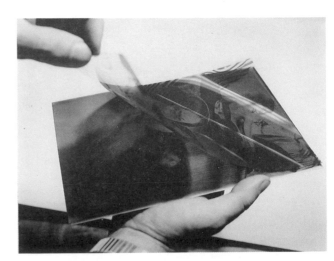

Above: Close-up of a lith film positive being laid with the dull surface contacting the gelatin emulsion.

Step Test Exposure for the Vacuum Frame Exposure Method

Below: After the lith film positive has been placed on top of the plate in the vacuum frame, expose the plate for time intervals ranging from 5 to 10 minutes. Then cover a third of the area of this plate by taping an opaque piece of cardboard to the outside of the vacuum frame and expose for a further interval of time. Then cover about two-thirds of the plate and repeat the process of exposure.

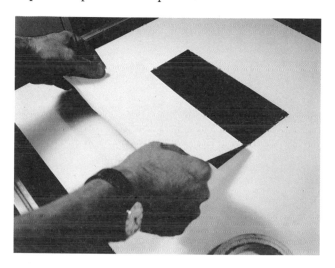

After the above exposure the emulsion on the plate will have darkened because of the action of the ultraviolet light and the stenciled image will be clearly visible.

At this point, a plate that is under or over-exposed will not be noticed until it is developed in hot water.

NB. A plate may look sufficiently exposed but when it is etched the emulsion may lift. This may be caused by humidity factors or **insufficient exposure.** If the emulsion lifts during the etching process increase the UV exposure before looking for other possible causes.

The vacuum frame method is by far the simplest and most predictable. In the absence of a vacuum frame the following described Wet Method can be tried but because gelatin absorbes moisture from the atmosphere this method will be more suited for drier climates. However, there is an additional step requiring a lot of trial and error, outlined on page 47, that can be taken to utilize the Wet Method in more humid environments.

The Wet Method of Exposing the Plate Without the Vacuum Frame.

An alternative method of contacting the lith film positive to the sensitized gelatin plate is the **wet method.** This involves taking a dry sensitized gelatin coated plate and the lith film positive and soaking it in cold water from 1 to 10 seconds. After this cold water pre-soaking take both the plate and the positive out of the water and squeegee them together with a photographic paper squeegee. This pre-soaking causes a change in the surface tension of the gelatin, allowing the lith film positive to stick to it.

Below: Submerging the dry sensitized gelatin coated plate and positive into cold water.

Below: Remove the plate and lith film positive from the pre-soaking bath and squeegee the excess water from between the lith film positive and the wet plate.

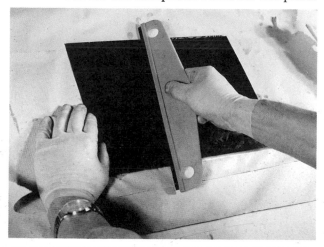

Gelatin, being anhydrous, will absorb moisture from the air. Thus the relative humidity in your studio must be taken into account when soaking the plate in the previously described <u>Wet Method</u>. If the gelatin is not sufficiently soaked the **lith film positive will pull the gelatin off the plate** when it is removed. If the gelatin contains too much moisture, through oversoaking or **atmospheric absorbtion**, the gelatin may melt under the heat of the exposing light and also pull off the plate. If the relative humidity is high you will have to do the pre-soak procedure in a **50% solution of 99% rubbing alcohol and water.** The plate should be left in this pre-soak alcohol solution for a period of 10 seconds to 1 minute before squeegeeing the lith film positive onto it. It is best to do some test plates to see which length of time and method is best suited to your particular atmospheric conditions.

After this initial pre-soaking step the lith film positive is ready to be squeegeed onto the surface of the gelatin coated plate after which it is ready to be exposed to whatever light source that you have elected to use.

After the plate has been exposed lift one corner of the lith film positive to determine if the gelatin has adhered to it. If it looks as though it is sticking try removing the lith film positive while it is completely submerged under **cold** water. The plate then should be quickly taken to the hot water bath for development.

Below: Removing the lith film positive from the submerged gelatin coated plate.

Developing the Plate

While the plate is being exposed, half fill a photo developing tray with hot water (120˚F).

Below: After exposure remove the lith film positive and drop the plate into the tray of hot water. Let the plate sit in the hot water for about 1 minute. After putting on a clean pair of rubber gloves start slowly and gently massaging, in a circular motion, the surface of the emulsion with two large cotton balls. This circular movement will cause the areas of the emulsion that were unaffected by light to dissolve.

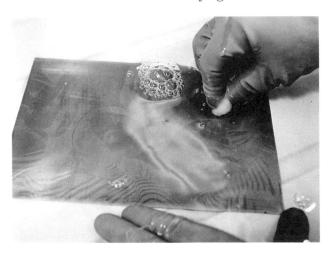

Below: This developing action should be carried out for about 5 minutes. The image from the stencil will become clearly visible.

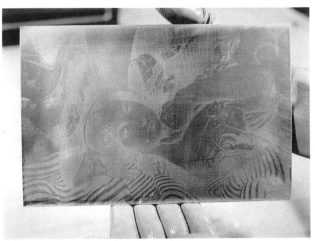

Take care not to rub the gelatin emulsion too hard or scratch it with your finger nails as this emulsion is quite soft and fragile.

Next, take the plate from the hot water development bath and spray it with cold water and then prop vertically to dry.

If the plate is left in direct sunlight the emulsion will harden further and promote speedy drying. Otherwise, submerge the plate in a bath of rubbing alcohol for one minute, after which the alcohol can be squeegeed off the plate and then the plate can be propped up in front of a a cool fan. Speed drying in this manner is not recommended if **extremely** fine detail is desired in the finished print. It is preferable to leave the plate to dry completely on its own accord.

Above: Etching by the author utilizing the "Howard Process". This image used an 85 line halftone and the plate was over-etched for 4 hours to the point where 3 holes where etched through the plate, see page 22.

Determining if the Plate is Under or Over Exposed

Below: If an 85 line halftone was used, and the plate was under exposed, the fine dot structure in the darkest areas will have washed away. This can easily be seen if the plate is examined at an angle to the light. Note that the emulsion at the top left hand area of the image below has washed away.

If the plate has been over exposed the dots in the light grey areas will start to fill in. Over exposure causes the light to creep under the dots of the half tone positive. The smaller the dot the more the likelihood of this occurring. This can be further verified by examining the plate with the magnifier.

If this test shows an under or over-exposure, then increase or decrease the exposure time until an optimum exposure is determined.

N.B. *When developing the plate in hot water it is important to be sensitive to the tactile surface of the plate. When the plate is first submerged into the hot water and the circular motion applied with the cotton balls the surface of the plate will feel slimy. This sliminess is due to the unexposed gelatin dissolving in the hot water and once this has completely dissolved the surface of the plate will have a completely different feel. If this sliminess persists throughout the developing process it is a good indication that the plate was under-exposed.*

I believe that it is very important to **attune yourself** to the subtleties within each technique and medium as it is these subtleties that are the indicators of whether or not each step has been completed successfully.

The Nature of the Etching Process

The etchant used in the "Howard Process" is ferric chloride. Ferric chloride is a very strong salt solution and can be purchased in premixed liquid form or made up from a powder.

The etching action of ferric chloride is slower than nitric acid, the most common etchant currently in use. **Solutions of nitric acid are highly corrosive and will produce severe burns to the skin and eyes. The fumes given off by nitric acid are corrosive to the skin, the mucous membranes, the eyes, nose and upper respiratory tract and to dental enamel. Breathing nitric acid fumes can also cause irreversible lung damage.**

Plates etched in nitric acid are more prone to undercutting. Undercutting occurs when the acid etches, not only down into the metal, but also sideways as it etches down.

The salt of iron in the ferric chloride has a strong corrosive effect on the copper that produces no fumes and, at worst, can be described as a skin and eye irritant.

In comparing both nitric acid and ferric chloride as etchants, ferric chloride is by far the superior not only in terms of its etching quality but also in terms of personal health and safety.

In conventional photogravure a number of different strength solutions of ferric chloride are used in succession to etch the plate. In the "Howard Process", only one etch and one strength of ferric chloride is required. The ferric chloride must have a strength between 42 and 50 Baume. (Baume is a measure of specific gravity or **density of liquids.** How to measure Baume will be discussed on page 53.)

In the "Howard Process", the gelatin emulsion acts primarily to selectively protect the copper plate from the corrosive effect of the ferric chloride.

In the other hand etched non-photo techniques, described in this book, the gelatin emulsion is replaced by water based ink, non wax acrylic floor finish or Hunt Speedball Water Soluable Screen Filler 4570.

Below: If the plate is left too long in the ferric chloride it will eventually eat right through the plate. This is a 200X enlargement of the top right hole of the plate illustrated on page 22.

If the plate is left in the ferric chloride solution for too long the ferric chloride eventually dissolves the fine gelatin dots that are in the blackest areas, and a terracing effect occurs. Not only is there a terracing effect but there is also a slight trough created within these terraces which, in the final print, creates a mezzotint type black.

At this point, because there is a slight breakdown of the gelatin emulsion by the ferric chloride, the "Howard Process" turns into a simplified type of photogravure.

Another technique where the surface ground is slowly destroyed by the ferric chloride, as it etches the plate, is the Lift-ground technique (page 80).

One further advantage the "Howard Process" has over the conventional photo etching processes is that the unpredictability of periodically pulling the plate out of the nitric acid, to progressively block it out by hand, is eliminated. Some artists dealt with this unpredictable quality by proofing and manipulating the plate during the etching cycle. For those artists who have developed their particular style through this progressive etching technique, it should not be too difficult for them to adapt to manipulating the plate after the main etch has been completed.

To the experienced printmaker, this unique technique has a new set of demands that requires reevaluating working methods, but **the greater flexibility, simplicity and personal safety afforded by the "Howard Process" should take their printmaking to new heights.**

A New Approach

The approach that the "Howard Process" takes focuses attention on solving visual esthetics problems in the darkroom, or in the hand preparation of stencils. Time spent here can save hours of reworking the etching plate.

Once the stencil is completed, it is feasible to produce a plate with a full range of image development in only one etch. By aiming at a higher level of finish from the first etch, it is possible to concentrate on the content of the image more than the process that makes it. This addresses a common criticism of printmakers in that they are often accused of being more concerned with the process of making prints rather than the finished results.

Technical virtuosity and diversity are still greatly valued assets for the printmaker. There is a direct ratio between the number of techniques available to the artist and to the number of creative possibilities that exist through the utilization of these techniques. **This book aims at giving the artist and photographer a completely new avenue of creative expression by expanding their present vocabulary of technical possibilities.**

After the first etch has been completed image adjustments may or may not be necessary . The option still remains to rework the plate using any or **all available** processes. The fact of the matter remains that, after the first main etch has been completed, the plate can be recoated with emulsion, re-exposed and re-etched if desired. The plate can be further reworked with any traditional technique or any of the other techniques described in this book.

Above: Etching, 9" x 12", by Ken Burkholder, made with tone drop-out and spray aquatint.

The Etching Tank

Although etching the plate in ferric chloride can be carried out in the photo developing tray, there are two disadvantages in using this type of tray.

The first relates to the large surface area of the tray that contributes to the rapid evaporation of the water from the ferric chloride.

The second relates to the nature of the etching process. If the plate is etched face up the residual iron deposit, formed as a result of the corrosive reaction between ferric chloride and the exposed copper plate, inhibits the clean etch of the image. This is not to say that the etch will produce unacceptable results but to etch the plate either upside down or in a vertical tank is more efficient,

Below: To etch the plate upside down, make a sling with packing tape and support sticks and hang the plate upside down in the ferric chloride by bridging the support sticks across the top lip of the developing tray.

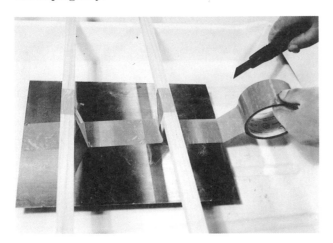

A New Design for Etching Tanks

The following tank is vertically oriented and is constructed from plexiglass and reinforced with fiberglass mesh and wood.

The dimensions of the tank should be determined by the range of plate sizes to be etched.

Vertical tanks will easily accommodate various sized plates. The tank dimensions for plates up to 9" x 12" is 14.5" high, 11" long and 1" wide.

The tank made for the 18" x 24" plate is 24" high, 26" long and 1" wide and will need 16 litres **(4 gal.)** of ferric chloride.

These tanks could have three internal 1" wide compartments, independently sealed from each other, that would allow more plates to be etched at one time (see illustration). Materials required include one eighth of an inch clear plexiglass, plexiglass cement, to assemble the component pieces, and a silicon type glue sealant ('Plumbers Goop' is excellent) to be used on all intersecting pieces of plexiglass.

Below: Sanding the edges prior to the application of the silicon sealant glue.

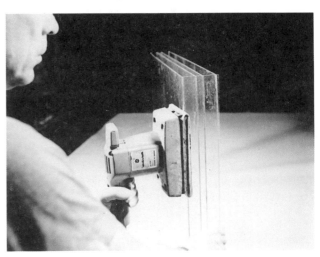

Below: After assembling the walls, fiberglass mesh and resin (purchased from the local hardware store) was applied to the external edges to completely seal and strengthen.

Below: Further support strength was added with wrap-around lengths of 2" x 2" pine and a lid made from corrugated plastic.

Below: Checking the specific gravity of the ferric chloride by floating a hydrometer in the vertical tank.

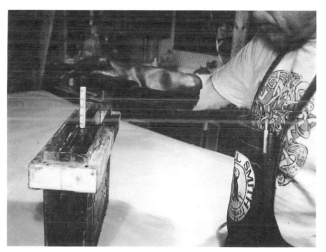

These tanks are ideal because:

1. Iron deposits formed in the etched areas of the plate fall to the bottom of the tank especially when used in conjuction with the aquarium air pump (see page 60).

2. They use workshop space more economically especially if they are slotted into the workbench so that the tank completely hangs below the top of the table and is covered with a hinged lid that, when closed, is flush with the top of the table.

3. Evaporation of water from the ferric chloride is also greatly reduced.

4. Convenient when testing the specific gravity of the ferric chloride with a hydrometer.

5. Convenient when emptying the tanks with the aid of a gasoline siphon (purchased from an auto accessory store).

Below: Test plate showing various divisions. The three prominent horizontal divisions, starting from the top of the plate moving to the bottom, were the result of lowering the plate upside down into an empty etching tank and cautiously adding ferric chloride. The top part of this plate was etched for 3 1/2 hours, the middle for 2 1/2 hours and the bottom for 1 1/2 hours. Between each layer it was a simple matter to add more ferric chloride.

The horizontal division that divides the plate in the middle was the result of exposing the gelatin emulsion on the left side for 5 minutes and the right side for 8 minutes.

The above test plate is further testimony to the extended etching latitude and flexibility of the "Howard Process".

Mixing and Testing the Ferric Chloride

Ferric chloride is purchased in a liquid or powder form. Purchasing it in liquid form is by far the safest. When mixing ferric chloride up from a powder it is essential that proper safety precautions are followed.

Sometimes it is necessary to add small quantities of ferric chloride powder to the commercial liquid preparation as some manufacturers of liquid ferric chloride do not add sufficient powder to meet the Baume strength measure indicated on the label. In other words, they water down the ferric chloride and sell it as a 42 Baume mix when in fact it is only 38 Baume. If a 38 Baume strength of ferric chloride is used in the "Howard Process" **it will lift the gelatin emulsion before the plate has finished its etching cycle** as the added water content partially dissolves the gelatin emulsion before the plate has completed its etch. This causes open biting of the plate, which basically alters and, in some cases, actually destroys any image that may be on the plate. On page *ix*, at the beginning of the book, Wendy Simon has utilized the disintegration effect of the watered down ferric chloride to create a unique image.

When purchasing ferric chloride avoid buying it in 500 gm (17.6 oz.) powdered lots or quart size bottles as this is the most expensive way of stocking up. Look for those companies that will sell it to you in greater quantities. Check with the suppliers listed on page 100 and 101 for the best current prices.

Testing with the Hydrometer

Because it is imperative that the density of the ferric chloride is known, a heavy liquid hydrometer with a Baume scale, is indispensable. A hydrometer is somewhat like a fishing float, as it is designed to float in liquids and the depth at which it sinks determines the density of that liquid. It looks like a test tube with a printed numbered scale ranging from 0-70 Baume inside, weighted down at one end with a small glob of mercury. The zero end of the scale is the Baume measure for water. Any liquids that exceed zero + are denser than water. This is why this particular type of hydrometer is classified as a heavy liquid hydrometer. The optimum temperature for measuring liquids with a hydrometer is 60F°.

Above: If the emulsion on the plate appears to have lifted, as above, it is the direct result of using a ferric chloride solution that contains too much water or a gelatin emulsion that has absorbed too much atmospheric humidity.

Above: Hydrometers come in many shapes and sizes. The best one to purchase is about 12" in length. (See chapter on purchasing materials, page 100.)

Mixing the Ferric Chloride Powder

When mixing the ferric chloride powder wear eye protection, respirator, rubber gloves, and work apron.

To make up 3.4 litres **(about 0.75 gal.)**, start with a large container, add 3 litres **(3 quarts)** of room temperature tap water. To this add 2 kilograms **(4.5 lbs.)** of powdered ferric chloride. **Do this slowly to avoid splashing.** Mix this solution with a wooden or plastic spoon. Let stand overnight as there is considerable heat given off while the ferric chloride is dissolving in the water.

Below: Adding the powdered ferric chloride to the distilled water.

Wait until the solution cools and check the specific gravity of this solution with the hydrometer. If the Baume reading is below 42, more ferric chloride powder should be added and a test plate made. If the emulsion falls off the plate increase the strength of the ferric chloride until a plate can be successfully etched.

Preparing Pre-mixed Ferric Chloride

Any pre-mixed ferric chloride solution should be tested with a hydrometer. If the reading is below 42 Baume, either put the ferric chloride into a photo tray in direct sunlight, to allow natural evaporation to occur, or add small quantities of powdered ferric chloride to the solution.

Remember that the optimum strength of the ferric chloride relates to the atmospheric humidity in your studio. If the humidity is high and the ferric chloride solution is reading 42 Baume and the gelatin emulsion prematurely falls off the plate during etching, the strength of the ferric chloride may need to be increased.

There is a perfect ratio of water to ferric chloride that you will have to discover for your particular situation.

Below: One way to add powdered ferric chloride is to put a pouring funnel into the neck of the original storage bottle and pour in some powdered ferric chloride, periodically testing with the hydrometer until the desired 42 Baume is reached. Eye protection, rubber gloves, respirator, and work apron must be used when carrying out this procedure.

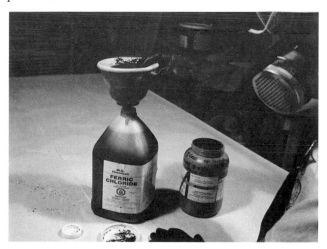

Plate Preparation Prior to Etching

Materials

1. A roll of self-adhesive vinyl covering such as Mac-Tac or Tye-Tac commonly used as shelf liners or book jacket protectors. There may be other similar products on the market that will equally serve the purpose.

2. Cutting blade.

3. Clean newsprint paper.

4. Large cotton balls.

5. A bottle of liquid acrylic floor finish.

6. A soft haired brush.

Plate Preparation

There are two excellent methods for sealing the back of the plate prior to etching. The first method uses Mac Tac, the second uses non wax liquid acrylic floor finish.

First method.

Cut a piece of Mac Tac about 1" larger, in both width and height, than the plate.

Below: Place the plate face down onto a clean piece of newsprint. Separate at one end the sticky plastic of the Mac Tac from its backing and attach this to the top end of the back of the plate. Simultaneously pull the backing off and adhere the Mac Tac by running your thumb from one side of the plate to the other.

When the backing is completely removed press the Mac Tac down with your thumb. Make sure that bubbles are pressed out towards the edges.

Trim the plate with a sharp blade, being careful **not to get finger marks onto the front side of the plate.** The trimmings can be used to make a lowering strap by taping to the middle of the back of the plate.

Second method.

Use a soft haired brush and paint a small amount of non wax acrylic floor finish onto the back of the plate until it is covered. (Non wax acrylic floor finish can be found on most supermarket shelves under the floor polish/cleaning section.) Add about 50 ml **(1 oz.)** of blue food colouring to the floor finish to make it easier to see when applying the floor finish. Make sure the floor finish does not spill around the edges as this will block out the image to be etched. Acrylic floor finish dries quickly. To be sure of complete coverage, a second coat is advised. Avoid getting finger prints onto the reverse side of the plate as this will retard the etching process.

The liquid acrylic floor finish is easily removed with a fifty percent mixture of water and household bleach. There are commercially made acrylic floor finish removers (without the smell of bleach) that are generally sold on the same shelves as the floor finish.

Below: Coating the back of the plate with liquid acrylic floor finish. (Floor finish illustrated has blue food colur added to make it more visible.)

Wendy Simon, diptytch, 12" x 9" utilizing the "Howard Process". A kodalith positive was made from a black and white negative and a fine mezzotint halftone screen. The plate was etched in a flat dish for 2.5 hours.

Etching the Plate

After the sensitized plate is exposed, developed, and the back sealed, it is ready to be etched. At this point the plate may have to go through a **pre-soaking water bath** before it is dropped into the ferric chloride tank for a prescribed length of time. This etching time will depend on the strength and temperature of the ferric chloride, the hardness of the copper plate used, the type of image to be etched and the desired finish. Although the plate can be etched in a still solution of ferric chloride a more efficient etch is obtained by etching the plate in a tank that has an aquarium air pump. This pump keeps the ferric chloride in constant motion over the surface of the plate as it etches (this is discussed in more detail on page 60).

The Pre-soaking Water Bath

The pre-soaking water bath is done to those gelatin coated plates that are made in studios that have a low relative humidity. The gelatin coated plate needs a certain amount of moisture before it will etch and the exact amount of moisture needed is not known.

When the relative humidity in the studio is low, one simple approach to the problem of whether to pre-soak the gelatin coated plate or not is to routinely pre-soak the plate prior to etching. (**However,** if a plate is pre-soaked unnecessarily it may lead to the gelatin lifting during the etching process.) If the plate has not been pre-soaked it should be pulled out of the ferric chloride, after about 30 minutes, to examine the surface of the plate to see if it has etched. When the ferric chloride has etched the copper plate a dark brown residue is noticeably left in those areas of the plate unprotected by the gelatin resist. If this brown residue is absent, wash the plate with cold running water for a second or two and then return it to the etching tank to restart the etching cycle. If the gelatin coated plate is left in the pre-soak water bath for more than a second or two it may also lead to the destruction of the gelatin coating before the etching cycle has been completed.

If the gelatin emulsion continues to lift (see page 53), before etching has completed, the next plate to be etched should be pre-soaked, for 3 seconds to 1 minute in a 50% solution of rubbing alcohol and water. It is best to make a test plate. The alcohol reduces the moisture content of the gelatin.

NB. If the gelatin emulsion prematurely lifts during the etching process you will have to clean and recoat the plate and **lengthen the UV exposure** before it can be etched again.

Below: Before submerging the plate in the ferric chloride make a simple hanging device that will allow easy removal of the plate from the etchant. This can be done by sticking a 1" length of Mac Tac or packing tape onto the back of the plate.

If the air pump is not used, stir the ferric chloride solution before immersing the plate. Also, dip the plate in and out a couple of times to make sure no air bubbles linger on the surface of the emulsion. If bubbles are allowed to remain on the emulsion during etching, these areas will not etch.

Determining the Length of the Etch

Using an 85 line halftone image and fresh ferric chloride at about 70°F, a good etching time for producing a full range of tones will be between 1.5 and 3 hours. If the temperature of the ferric chloride is higher then 70°F or if an air pump is used, the etching time will be less.

For a hard-ground line drawing (see page 73) 20 to 40 minutes is sufficient etching time to give a black line.

Aquatints (page 71), either the rosin or spray type, can have etching times from a few seconds to 3 hours. It is important to realize that a great diversity of results can be achieved through controlling and understanding the consequences of etching time. Experience is the best determining factor.

How to Control
Tonality and Contrast

Tonality in this regard refers to the possible range of tones that exist between white and black. **Two factors** affect tonality and contrast of the finished print:

The first; is the length of time the gelatin emulsion is exposed to the ultraviolet light.

The second; is the length of time the image is etched.

It is important to appreciate the great degree of flexibility in both these factors. It is possible to produce as many as 10 different acceptable results from one halftone image. The difference between these 10 images will be the range of tonalities and the contrast in each. The longer the plate is allowed to etch, the greater the contrast and the lower the tonality. Tonality and contrast are also increased by over exposing the plate to the ultraviolet light source.

The **above** prints show different tonal ranges. The etching on the left shows less contrast and more muted greys as a result of a 2 hour 30 minute etch in fresh ferric chloride. The etching on the right shows a greater contrast and less muted greys and was etched for 3 hours 15 minutes. It should be noted that etching times will also vary according to how old the ferric chloride is.

The **above** prints, by Roslyn De Mille, were etched for 3 and 12 hours (done in a still solution of ferric chloride) respectively showing not only a great change in contrast but also in the nature of the finished image.

Below: Lowering the etching plate into the ferric chloride tank. It is a good practice to note the time the plate was emersed into the ferric chloride onto the top portion of the hanging device.

Below: Onc method of checking the depth of the bite is to probe the surface of the plate with an etching needle. Eventually you will learn how deep to bite the plate from the feel of the surface texture.

Above: Blaine Ruttan, etching 9" x 12". This print was made from an 85 line halftone image in conjunction with the spray coating method, outlined on page 38. The spray coating technique imparts an aquatint look to any image used.

Making the Etching Process More Efficient

One inexpensive way of improving the efficiency of the actual etching process is to convert an aquarium air pump in such a way that a constant stream of air bubbles flow across the surface of the plate during the etching process.

Most aquarium air pumps push a constant stream of air through a plastic tube that is attached to an air stone to weigh it down. To convert this pump for use in the etching tank, use the following materials:

1. Wire clothes hanger.

2. Aquarium air pump.

3. Plastic tubing to fit the aquarium air pump.

4. Etching needle and cigarette lighter.

5. Pliers and black electrician's tape.

6. In-line electrical on/off switch.

Converting the Air Pump

1. **Below:** Cut the coat hanger wire into one continuous length and thread a piece of the plastic tubing onto it.

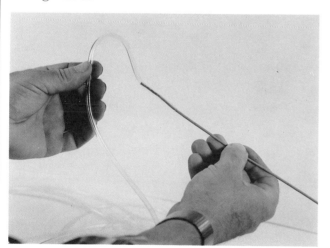

As this wire will eventually be the support for the perforated tubing it is necessary to completely seal it from the corrosive attack of the ferric chloride.

2. **Below:** To completely seal the coat hanger wire, melt each end of the tubing using a cigarette lighter and seal shut with pliers.

3. **Below:** To make a single tank support, bend the above described wire so that it fits across the bottom of the tank and up the side walls. It is possible to double up on the above single tank support so that the support wire can also be bent in one continuous length to fit into the adjacent tank. (This will require using more than one coat hanger.)

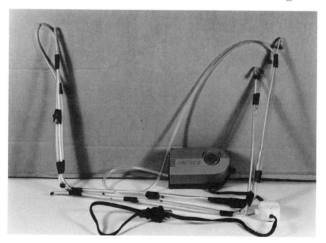

4. Seal one end of a separate length of tubing by melting it in the manner previously described.

5. Attach this continuous length of tubing to the support with black electrical tape.

6. **Below:** Perforate the length of tubing that will lay at the bottom of the tank with small holes. This can best be accomplished by heating an etching needle with a cigarette lighter and melting holes at about 3" intervals.

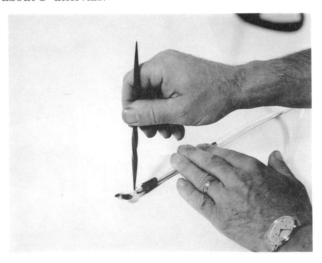

7. **Below:** At this point it is important to check the air flow through the tubing by submerging it into a tank of water and turning on the pump.

8. **Below:** Attach the in-line on/off switch to the cord of the air pump. As these pumps are normally made to be left on continuously, an in-line switch will be helpful as it is only necessary to turn it on when the plate is etching.

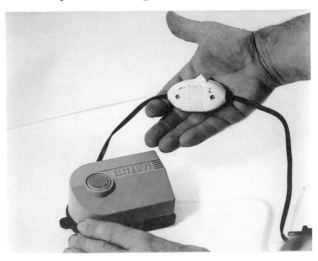

9. **Below:** Pressure fit the support wire to fit onto the lip of the top of the etching tank.

As the air pump creates a lot of surface bubbles it is advisable not to fill the tank completely to the top with the ferric chloride solution.

Aquarium stores also sell a plastic control valve that when attached to the air hose can control the surface bubbles. This control valve also comes in handy to control the overall agitation within the tank. Sometimes too much agitation can cause over-biting of the plate.

After the Etch

After the plate has completed its etch, remove it to the washing-out sink and thoroughly wash off the ferric chloride residue with a strong jet of hot water. The hot water will completely or partially remove the gelatin emulsion remaining on the plate. **If the gelatin falls off the plate without any resistance**, with only a light spray of hot water, it is an indication that the ferric chloride has too much water in it or the moisture content of the gelatin emulsion was too high. This moisture content may be too high due to atmospheric humidity or over soaking in the pre-soak water bath. Remember that there is an alternative to the pre-soak water bath and that is to pre-soak the gelatin coated plate, for a few seconds up to 1 minute, in a bath containing 50% alcohol and 50% water. It is also possible to increase the strength of the alcohol. **Alcohol effectively reduces the moisture content of the gelatin.**

If the gelatin emulsion continues to lift more ferric chloride powder should be added to the existing ferric chloride solution or allow some of the water to evaporate. This reduces the water content of the ferric chloride.

Gelatin that refuses to budge can be removed in three ways:

1. If time permits, let the plate stand overnight and most of the gelatin will fall off on its own accord (this method works only in studios with low humidity).

2. Submerge the plate into a bath of undiluted household bleach. This action will remove the emulsion very quickly. The tray containing the bleach should be covered with a piece of plexiglass.

3. The plate can be scrubbed with a nylon pot scrubber and Comet cleanser.

Remember, if the gelatin emulsion falls off the plate too easily it is an indication that either, the ferric chloride has too much water in it, or, the gelatin emulsion has absorbed too much moisture from the atmospheric humidity.

Final Plate Preparation Before Printing

After the emulsion has been completely removed, squeegee excess water off the plate and wipe with paper toweling until completely dry. If the self adhesive vinyl backing was applied to the back of the plate, this should be removed. If the non wax acrylic floor covering was used it is not necessary to remove this.

If 20 gauge copper plate is used, it will be necessary to round off the sharp corners with a small metal file. The corners are rounded off to prevent them from snagging during the tarlatan wiping procedure (page 66). Thicker plates should also have a small 45° bevelled edge to prevent cutting into the press blankets.

Above, etching 9" x 12", by Barbara McSween. A sensitized gelatin coated plate was exposed to dried plants and developed in hot water. The plate was spray aquatinted using the Hunt Speedball screen filler 4570 and then etched for 1 hour. After which the background was made with the Screen Filler Lift Ground Method outlined on page 80.

Printing the Plate

The Intaglio Printing Process

To understand the nature of this printing process it is important to realize that the reason the plate was etched by ferric chloride was to create pits, grooves and valleys below the surface of the plate. There is a printing technique called *intaglio* in which these pits, grooves and valleys can be filled with ink after which the ink particles, on the top surface of the plate, are wiped away leaving the top surface of the plate clean. Through the aid of an etching press, etching paper can be pressed onto the plate forcing the ink, left in the valleys and grooves, to transfer to the paper, resulting in a print.

Printing Equipment and Materials

1. An Etching press is mandatory.

2. Etching ink.

3. Tarlatan.

4. Glass mixing palette and palette knife.

5. Gloves for inking.

6. Etching paper.

7. Tray of water to soak the paper.

9. Blotting paper.

10. Small pieces of card.

11. Vegetable oil.

See materials source section, page 102.

Presetting the Etching Press

Below: The etching press is constructed with a flat bed that rolls between two large rollers under controllable pressure.

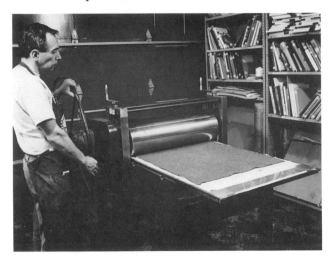

The inked plate is placed on this etching press bed, dampened paper is positioned on top of the plate, and then three felt blankets cover the paper.

The plate and paper are sandwiched between the press bed and the felt blankets and a print is taken by rolling this press bed, under tremendous pressure, between the rollers.

Below: The three felt blankets used to cover the printing paper are called the pusher (compacted top felt blanket), the cushion (softer middle felt) and sizing catcher (thin felt to absorb excess water from the wet etching paper).

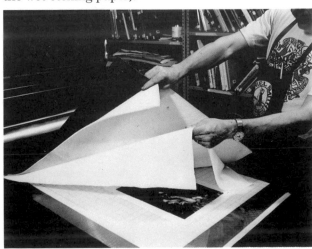

For those experienced printmakers who have used etching presses, the pressure needed to print these copper plates is slightly more than the pressure needed for a conventional etching. For those doing this for the first time the best pressure will be ascertained through trial and error.

The printing press should be set before proceeding to the inking and wiping stage.

A good starting procedure for correctly setting the pressure of the etching press is as follows:

Below: Start by off setting the pusher blanket (top blanket) from the cushion and soaker blankets by a few inches and positioning the top roller of the etching press onto the cushion blanket.

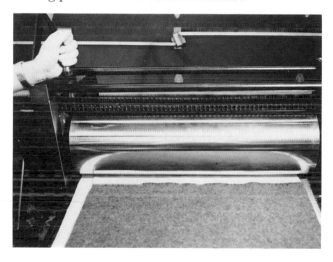

Roll the etching bed through the rollers. It is very important to develop a sensitivity to the pressure of the press as it is transmitted through to the cranking or turning handle. The pressure of the press changes with different thicknesses of plates, paper and with a change of etching blankets.

Below: A dry run, using an un-inked plate and dampened paper, will be a good indicator in determining the correct press pressure. After the plate and paper have been run through the press, the paper should have a very noticeable plate embossing mark.

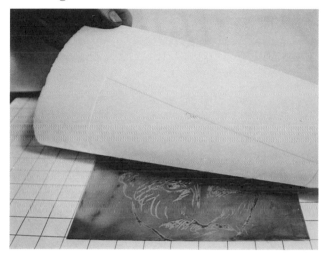

The Inking and Wiping Technique

There are several different techniques used for hand printing etching plates. The technique described here was chosen because it is one of the safest and easiest.

The tarlatan is a stiff cheesecloth type fabric used to wipe ink from the plate. The stiffness should first be taken out by washing the tarlatan briefly in warm water and hanging it up to dry.

The entire inking and wiping process should be carried out wearing solvent resisting rubber gloves.

Deposit a small quantity of etching ink onto the glass palette and fold several times with the palette knife. This conditions the ink.

Etching ink varies in stiffness according to the manufacturer. There are ink additives that can reduce the stiffness of the ink. The stiffer the ink the more difficult it is to wipe off the plate.

Five of the most common ink additives include Sureset, Burnt Plate Oil, Setswell, Easy-wipe and Daniel Smith Miracle Reducer. These products, when added in small proportions of between 2% and 10% of the quantity of ink, help create a satisfactory working consistency and short, smooth dispersion of ink. Determining what and how much ink additive to add to the etching ink is, to a certain degree, determined by printing experience and individual circumstances. If, for instance, a plate has an extremely delicate shallow bitten line it may need a stiff ink to print it successfully.

Ink dries due to its exposure to oxygen and once a can of etching ink has been opened it should be sealed again in such a way as to prevent the exposed top layer of ink from drying and developing a "skin". Two methods are recommended to prevent this:

First: Before putting the can away, spray the top layer of ink with Anti-Skin spray (a brand name for a spray that prevents the surface of the ink from drying).

Second: Specially prepared skin papers can be used instead of the Anti-Skin spray. Be sure to smooth out any air bubbles that may have become trapped under the skin paper.

Inking the Plate

Below: Etching ink is squeegeed onto the surface of the plate with a piece of card. Scrape the ink-laden card across the surface of the plate at an angle of about 45 degrees. This will force the ink into the valleys and grooves of the plate.

Below: If this is done correctly, the etched image will be quite noticeable and only a small layer of ink should remain. This residue layer of ink is removed with the tarlatan cloth in such a manner as not to disturb the ink below the surface.

Below: Ruffle a three foot square of tarlatan into a pad and, with continuous wipes, slowly remove the ink until the top surface is visibly clean.

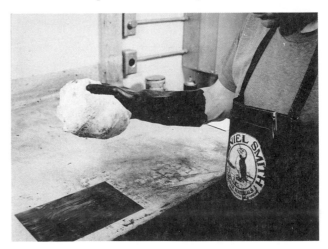

This wiping process is an acquired skill. Learning when a plate is under or over wiped is a matter of experience and involves developing the ability to "read the plate" (determining how much ink is being removed through continuous visual monitoring) during the wiping process.

Wiping the Etching Plate

The wiping action can best be described as a long sweeping action that continues from one side of the plate to the other and is first done with an old ink-laden tarlatan, finishing with a cleaner tarlatan pad. One hand wipes the plate, and the other controls and rotates the plate during wiping.

1.

3.

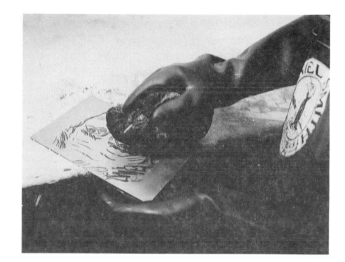

2.

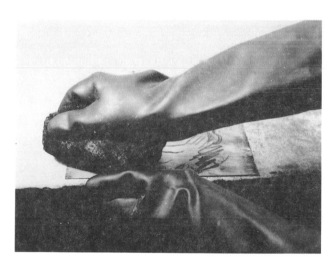

4.

Correctly wiping plates requires a special touch. One of the most important aspects of successfully wiping plates is to be a keen observer of the subtle changes of ink on the surface of the plate as it is being wiped.

The Etching Paper

The Etching Paper and its Preparation

100 percent rag etching paper produces the best results. This paper should be soaked in a dish of water prior to printing to soften the paper, allowing the pressure of the printing press to force the paper into the inked plate and transfer the ink to the paper.

The length of time the paper can be soaked will depend on the type of rag paper used. Good quality rag paper can be soaked for as little as 1 minute or as long as 24 hours. B.F.K. Rives is an excellent all-round printmaking paper, needing only to be soaked for ten minutes prior to printing. This paper can also be soaked for several hours before printing without any ill effect. There are many fine grade papers suitable for etching. Further advice can be sought from the art supply store that sells the paper or directly from the paper manufacturer.

Below and right: Laying the dampened paper between blotters and removing the excess moisture. A rolling pin can also be used on top of the blotters to aid with the blotting procedure. A sheet of plastic placed on top of the blotters will prolong the life of the blotters.

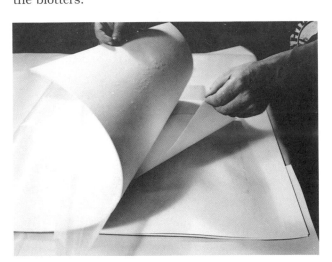

The wet paper is placed between two sheets of blotting paper to remove excess moisture. If the paper is too wet or too dry, the ink will not transfer successfully. Some printmakers substitute unprinted newsprint for blotting paper. Others hang the paper, prior to wiping, and by the time it is ready to be printed the paper will have reached the perfect degree of dampness.

Paper Handling Procedure

If unwanted ink marks on the printing paper are to be avoided, a strict handling routine is advised. **The routine is simple: Only touch the etching plate and wiping materials with a gloved hand and only touch the printing paper, etching blankets and etching press with an ungloved hand.**

The Printing Procedure

1. **Below:** The inked plate is positioned on the etching bed (wearing gloves).

2. **Below:** Remove gloves and cover the inked plate with the dampened paper.

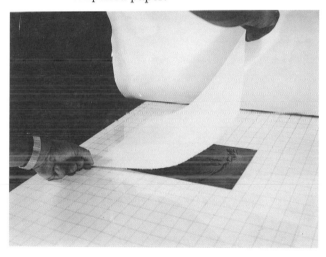

3. **Below:** Lay the blankets over the paper .

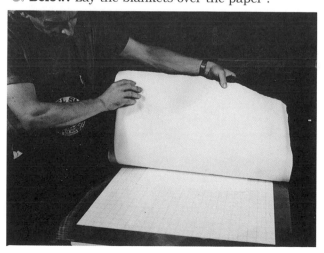

4. **Below:** Turn the wheel of the etching press which forces the etching bed through the rollers.

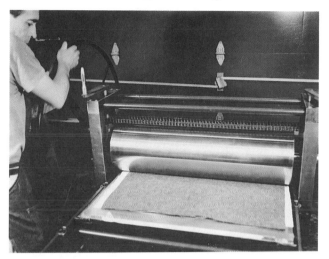

5. **Below:** Fold back the blankets and remove the print.

6. Lay the print onto a clean surface to dry.

7. Put gloves back on, remove plate from etching bed and wipe bed with clean rag.

The entire process must be repeated for successive prints.

The plate and inking area can be cleaned by dropping a small quantity of **vegetable oil** on to these areas and wiping with a rag. An oily residue should remain on the plate. The plate can be wrapped with cling wrap or further cleaning can be done with Hanco or Luster Sheen hand cream cleaner followed by a final wiping with Fantastik all purpose cleaner.

"Open Biting"

"Open biting" occurs when areas of the plate, thicker than a pencil lead, are left bare allowing access for the ferric chloride to bite the plate. To completely understand "open biting", it is important to fully understand the nature of the inking, wiping and printing process. The ink must have something to hold it onto the plate, otherwise it will be wiped away by the tarlatan. Ink will remain in finely incised lines without fear of being wiped out, but as the line gets thicker the ink is held only by the extreme edges of the line.

The ink in the center of the line will wipe away and the resulting print will show a whitening of the thick line towards its center.

Controlled "open biting" can be used as a technique by itself, but if it occurs by accident, the image on the plate may be partially destroyed. If "open biting" is to be controlled, a **secondary process** of adding a dot structure must be carried out. This process is called **aquatint,** (see page 71).

Above: The gelatin coated plate after a brushed-on ink drawing was exposed and developed.

Above: Print made from the etched plate at left. This demonstrates the loss of ink in the open areas.

Above: Etching, 6"x 4", by Joann Murdock that utilized the liquid acrylic hard ground method, outlined on page 73, followed by the aquatint method outlined on page 71. The plate was finally burnished to bring out the highlights in the face.

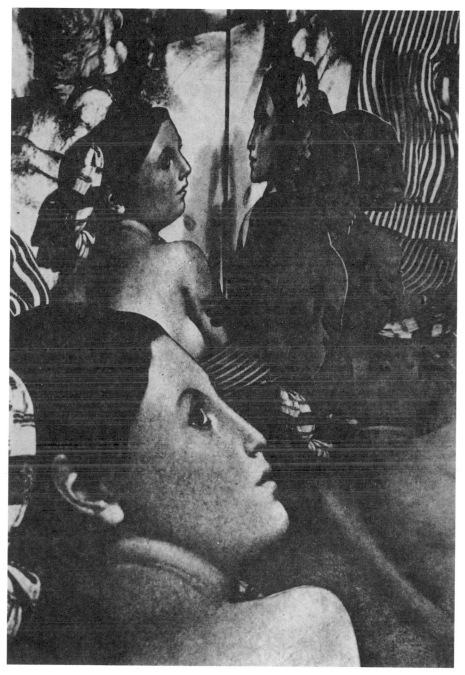

Above: An example, by the author, of an 85 line halftone image that was put onto the plate with the dip coating method. The same halftone screen was used for the image on page 72.

The Aquatint Method

The Aquatint

The traditional aquatint method consists of applying a rosin dust or powdered asphaltum to the surface of the etching plate. Rosin and asphaltum particles are melted onto the plate with the aid of a hot plate or propane torch, creating a uniformly speckled, acid resistant texture. When this is etched, a sandpaper-like surface results.

If this sandpaper-like texture is etched into the open areas of the plate, the ink will have a place to cling, making it difficult for the tarlatan to wipe away.

Unfortunately, rosin and powdered asphaltum aquatint have several hazards associated with their use.

The first: dusts created from both are volatile and if these dusts come in contact with a spark, an explosion can occur.

The second: this method requires some type of heat source to melt the dust, either a hot plate or propane torch. Both are fire hazards and can offer opportunities for burn injuries.

The third: the dust particles, if inhaled, are not metabolized by the body and can eventually cause severe lung irritation.

Above: Close-up of a plate sprayed with the Hunt Speedball Water Soluble Screen Filler. NB. Best results occur if the plate is etched in a still bath of ferric chloride as the air pump action can remove the small droplets of screen filler spray and lead to open biting.

A Safer Method of Aquatinting

The safest method of all is to use the sprayed gelatin emulsion (see page 40) or substitute the gelatin with **Hunt Speedball Water Soluble Screen Filler 4570.** This makes the richest aquatint. The screen filler needs diluting with about one third water to obtain a good spraying consistency. The greatest variety of aquatints, from coarse to very fine, can be achieved with this method according to how much the screen filler is diluted with water. The sprayed gelatin emulsion can be substituted for the screen filler and produces a range of results according to how much is sprayed onto the plate. This type of aquatint must be sun-hardened for at least 15 minutes before being etched.

If you do not own an air brush the next best alternative is a water-based acrylic spray can of enamel, the type that has been labeled "environmentally safe", available from the local hardware store. (Using a respirator and spraying in a vented area is still recommended for **any spray application**.)

Whatever spray method is used, the aim is to produce an even, overall spray coating. The size of the spray particle will determine its coverage. This coverage should be about 50% but can vary for different results. Be careful as it is possible to over or under spray the plate. This is something that will require some trial and error to determine differing results.

Creating Tonality with the Aquatint

If an even aquatint spray has been deposited onto the etching plate, each particle of spray will resist the ferric chloride etch. The longer the plate remains in the etchant, the deeper it will bite and the deeper the etch, the more ink will be contained. If a series of tones is desired, the plate must be etched for differing lengths of time, selectively blocking out the aquatinted areas between each segment of time. (see page 21). This creates various tonalities according to the length of time of each etch. The longer the etch, the darker the tone. The safest and simplest type of block-out for this purpose is the **Hunt Speedball Water Soluble Screen Filler 4570** (the type used in conjunction with the water based screen printing inks). Always degrease the plate before aquatinting (see page 31).

An area aquatinted by any of the previous methods can be etched in fresh ferric chloride for 40 or 50 minutes to make a black and as little as 30 seconds to make a faint grey. If a number of tonal variations is desired, the aquatinted plate should be etched for an interval of time, taken from the ferric chloride, dried and **undiluted** screen filler or liquid acrylic floor finish painted onto a preselected area. Then the plate is re-etched for a further interval of time, taken out, dried and re-etched.

This progressive method of blocking out and etching can be carried on for as many tonalities as desired. Those areas designated as being the blackest can be made richer by repeating the aquatinting procedure and re-etching the plate.

Before printing, the screen filler is easily removed with Comet pots and pans cleanser or by any number of liquid household cleaners such as Wisk or Mr. Clean.

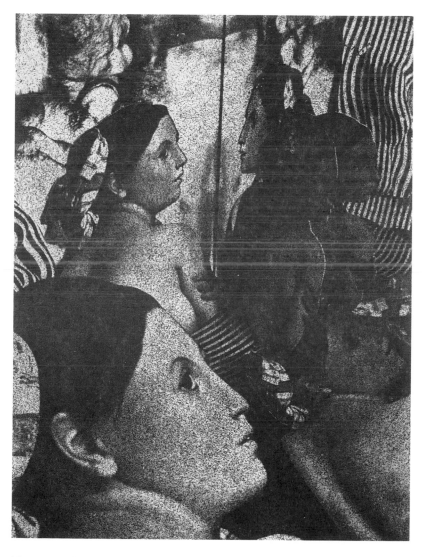

Above, etching, by the author, used the same 85 line halftone sceen shown on page 70. The difference between the above image and that on page 70 was created by the spray-coating of gelatin onto the plate. (See page 59 for a further example by Blaine Ruttan.)

New Approach to Hard and Soft-Ground

A New Look at Hard-Ground

Hard-ground is a term given to one of the simplest of etching techniques. The traditional hard-ground involves coating a metal plate with an acid-resistant coating consisting of a mixture of asphaltum and bees wax. This type of hard-ground is oil-based and requires the use of paint thinner, which is a health hazard.

One excellent alternative to the traditional hard-ground is the non-wax liquid acrylic floor finish found on the shelves of most supermarkets. In Canada, Future, Dura Shine, and Bravo are common brand names for these floor finishes and they come with their respective floor finish removers.

Applying the Hard-Ground

Thoroughly clean the copper plate with Comet cleanser and pot scrubber.

Below: After the plate is dry, stand it vertically in an empty photo tray and pour the acrylic floor finish at the top end of the plate, allowing it to flow down with sufficient quantity to completely cover the plate. If bubbles form, keep pouring until they are pushed to the bottom of the plate.

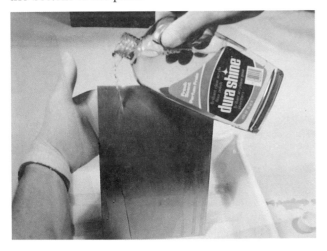

After the plate is coated return the excess overflow of floor finish to its bottle and leave the plate upright to dry. The photo tray then should be washed in running water.

Using the Hard-Ground

After the plate is completely coated with the acrylic floor finish, it is impervious to the corrosive attack of the ferric chloride. If this coating is removed by scratching with an etching needle or similar sharp point, the metal under the coating will be exposed. A drawing can thus be scratched into this floor finish, exposing the copper plate which then can be etched and printed.

Because the acrylic floor finish is transparent it is difficult to see the drawing as it is being drawn onto the copper plate. One simple solution is to either add 50 ml (**1 oz.**) of blue food colouring or paint Pelican's India Ink *for fountain pens* directly onto the dried floor finish.

Below: Adding a bottle of Pelican India Ink (for fountain pens) to the acrylic floor finish.

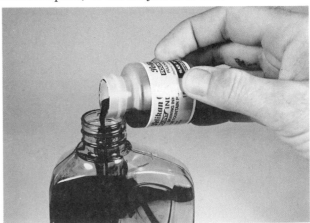

Mac Tac or two coatings of acrylic floor finish are then used to seal the back of the plate to prevent that side from being etched. The plate then can be dropped into a ferric chloride bath for a predetermined length of time, etched, inked and printed to make a hard-ground etching.

The length of time the plate is to etch will depend upon the desired tonal variety of the line.

As with the "Direct Negative" method (page21) the lines created by the scratching can be individually etched and progressively blocked out to achieve differing tonalities of lines. The best block-out to use is the Hunt Speedball Water Soluble Screen Filler (undiluted).

The Water-Soluble Relief-Ink Ground

Another excellent hard-ground is the water-soluble relief ink made by the Graphic Chemical and Ink Company (see page 105.) This relief ink makes a very unique type of hard-ground as the line produced will vary depending on how long the ink is left on the plate.

Applying the Relief-Ink Ground

The plate must be prepared in the same manner as described in the section 'Preparing the Copper Plate' (page 31).

1. The plate must be sanded with 320 grit wet and dry sandpaper.

2. The plate is then degreased with Comet cleanser. (Comet is a trade name for a pots and pans powdered cleanser.)

3. **Below:** Remove a small quantity of ink with a spatula and lay down a line of ink about the same size as the roller.

4. Roll up a pad of ink until there is an even, smooth consistency.

It is important when rolling up the pad of ink to allow the roller to leave the pad at the end of each pass and spin slightly. This results in a more even coating of ink onto the roller.

5. **Below:** Applying the Graphic Chemical relief ink to the the dry, degreased copper plate.

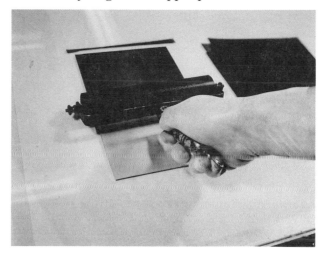

6. **Below:** The first layer will not be enough to completely cover the plate; several more thin layers, laid on in a criss-cross manner, will be needed .

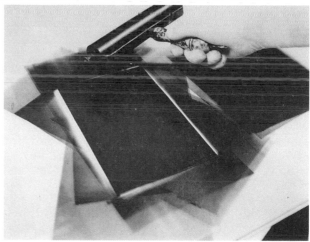

If a thin layer of ink is left on the plate for more then a few days before being etched, an uneven pitting will occur similar to a coarse aquatint. Some artists may wish to exploit this effect.

It is possible to draw directly into this wet layer of ink, but it will be necesary to wait at least 12 hours for the plate to dry completely before etching it.

Hard and Soft-Ground : Continued

Above: Etching made with the dried relief-ink ground.

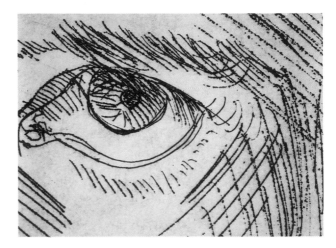

Above: Close-up of the unique line created with the relief-ink ground.

If you wait the 12 hours before scratching into the relief-ink ground, the nature of the line created will be totally different to any presently known technique. Because the relief-ink ground is slightly brittle, an etching needle breaking through fractures it, creating a very fine saw-tooth type line.

After the relief-ink ground drawing is completed the plate can be etched for any length of time. This time should be judged according to how black the final etching will be. If a black line is desired, an etching time of 45 minutes should be sufficient. If a tonal variety in the line is desired, lines can be etched, blocked out and re-etched. The best block out for this purpose is the **undiluted** Hunt Speedball Screen Filler 4570 or liquid acrylic floor finish. If, for instance, a very light line is desired, the plate is submerged into the ferric chloride for only 30 seconds, after which it is removed, washed off and dried. The line or lines that you wish to remain the lightest will now be blocked out with a brush and Hunts Speedball Water Soluble Screen Filler. Once the screen-filler is dry the plate can be returned to the ferric chloride for further degrees of etching and blocking out.

After the plate is completely etched the relief-ink can be removed by soaking the plate in a bath of household bleach for 15 minutes. If there is a slight residue of ink left on the plate, put on your rubber gloves and scrub the plate with hot water, pot scrubber and some Comet cleanser.

Below: A 200 X magnification of lines created with the dried relief ground on top of thinner lines created with the acrylic floor finish.

The Soft-Ground

*The **traditional** soft-ground is made by mixing one part tallow or grease to three parts of hard-ground. This is applied to a metal plate, creating a surface that is very pressure sensitive. Objects such as feathers, cloth, plant material and crumpled paper could be arranged onto the surface of the plate, then covered with a wax paper and run through the etching press.*

*A major problem with the **traditional** method is that the blankets and expensive press rollers can be damaged by objects such as coins, metal cans, bottle caps, spoons, etc. The pressure of the press transfers through the felt blankets onto these objects, after which the wax paper and objects are removed. An impression is left in the soft ground by the objects and it is this impression that can be etched and eventually printed.*

1. **Below:** A far simpler and easier method is to place the intended soft-ground objects directly onto a plate coated with the sensitized gelatin emulsion, then expose, develop, aquatint, etch and print.

3. **Below:** Close-up of the sprayed aquatint.

2. **Above:** Aquatinting the developed plate with air brush and Hunt's Water Soluble Screen Filler.

4. **Above:** The resulting print after the plate was etched for 45 minutes.

Another **traditional** application of the soft-ground method is to lay a thin piece of paper on top of the ground and draw on this paper with an HB pencil. The pressure of the pencil causes the ground to transfer to the paper, and when the paper is removed, the soft ground is taken with it, leaving an impression of the drawing behind. This impression can be etched and printed, creating a soft pencil-like etching.

The main problem with this method is that the drawing must be done without touching the thin paper with the drawing hand. If anything else touches the paper besides the pencil, extra marks will occur. Also, if there is not enough pressure put on the pencil, an insufficient amount of ground is removed, resulting in areas that will not etch. If too much pressure is given to the pencil it may rip through the thin paper causing further unwanted marks.

Duplicating the soft-ground effect can easily be done by drawing onto a piece of architect's tracing paper (drafting film) with a 3B pencil, thus creating a stencil that can be directly contacted onto the sensitized gelatin emulsion, exposed, etched and printed.

Another very successful method of making a direct stencil from a drawing is to photocopy it and make the photocopy transparent by rubbing vegetable oil onto the surface. Vegetable oil makes any photocopy transparent and usable as a stencil.

Below: Rubbing vegetable oil onto photocopy.

Below: An etching made directly from a 3B pencil drawing onto drafting film that was exposed to a gelatin-coated plate and etched.

Below: The result of first photocopying the drawing and making it transparent with vegetable oil and exposing it to a gelatin-coated plate and etched.

Printing Intaglio and Relief Together

One printing method that opens up a new set of creative possibilities is printing the etching plate intaglio and relief at the same time.

Materials

All the materials outlined in the section "Printing the Plate" on page 63 will be needed, in addition to the following materials :

1. Oil based relief printing ink.

2. Good quality relief roller.

3. Glass inking-up slab.

4. Stiff acetate or polyester.

5. Sharp cutter.

6. Fine pointed marker.

7. Masking tape.

Following is a description of the intaglio relief printing method that utilizes an acetate stencil that isolates particular areas on the plate to be relief inked. If the entire plate is to be relief-inked the acetate is not used.

Intaglio and Relief Printing Method

1. Prior to inking-up the plate, a stiff piece of acetate or polyester is laid onto the etching plate and the area to be isolated from the relief roll is marked with a fine pointed felt-tipped marker.

2. The isolated area on the acetate is then cut out with a sharp cutter.

3. The **oil based** relief ink is then rolled out onto the inking-up slab similar to the method outlined on page 74, "The Water-Soluble Relief-Ink Ground". An oil based relief ink is used instead of the water based ink, because, after the plate is inked intaglio with an oil based etching it will leave a greasy plate surface which would resist any water based relief ink.

4. The plate is then inked in the intaglio method outlined in the section "Printing the Plate" on page 63.

5. **Below:** The acetate stencil is taped into position on top of the plate.

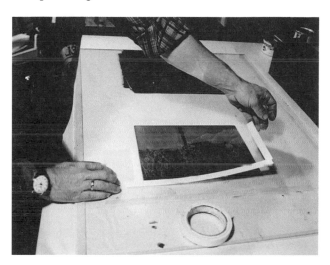

6. **Below:** The relief ink is then rolled onto the plate. One or more layers can be applied. Be careful as the roller will want to pull the acetate stencil off the plate.

7. **Below:** After the relief ink has the desired covering the acetate stencil is removed.

8. The plate is then printed as outlined in the section "Printing the Plate" on page 63.

This technique can be successfully combined with any other technique outlined in this book. One interesting variation of this technique is to roll up a blend of colours and apply that to the plate. Blending colours basically involves laying small amounts of coloured oil based relief inks side by side onto the roll-up slab. The roller is then rolled onto the coloured inks until all the colours blend evenly together. Also, a special transparent base, available from the ink manufacturer, when added to the relief ink can produce very subtle tones.

The **above** etching, 9" x 12", by Blaine Ruttan, was made from a tone drop-out that was spray aquatinted and etched.

Above: The same etching on the left after being printed intaglio and relief at the same time.

Screen Filler Lift-Ground

The screen filler lift-ground is a very unique and flexible method of making etchings that simulate brush marks. It is possible to achieve a full range of tonality, after only one etch, by brushing the diluted screen-filler onto the degreased surface of the etching plate.

Materials

1. Hunt Speedball Water Soluble Screen Filler number 4570.

2. A variety of painting brushes.

3. Comet cleanser and scrubbing pad.

4. Paper towel.

The Lift-Ground

This technique is probably one of the simplest techniques in this book but requires some trial and error proofs to become familiar with the subtleties and extreme diversity of marks that are possible.

If the copper plate has some unwanted surface scratches they should be removed with 320 grit wet-and-dry sandpaper before degreasing. (See page 31.)

The first step is to thoroughly degrease the copper plate with Comet cleanser.

The second step is to dilute the Hunt Speedball Screen Filler Number 4570 with approximately one third water (the dilution can vary considerably for different results). I use the same dilution for the spray aquatint method outlined on page 71. This diluted screen filler is then simply brushed onto the plate, allowed to dry and subsequently etched in a **still** (turn air pump off) 42 Baume ferric chloride solution for up to three hours. Any exposed areas of the plate will "open bite" (see page 69).

If "open biting" is to be prevented this technique can be used in conjunction with the aquatint process described on page 71. In fact to spray aquatint the plate, after the initial brush covering of screen filler, will result in an entirely different print.

Below: This plate was brushed with the diluted screen-filler 4570 and the left side was spray aquatinted with the same filler then etched in ferric chloride for about 3 hours.

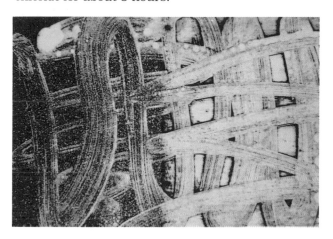

Below: This plate was brushed with a diluted screen-filler and etched (without aquatint) for 3 hours.

This method works in a similar way as does photogravure. The ferric chloride progressively breaks through the screen-filler to etch the plate. The thicker the screen-filler appears on the surface of the plate the lighter that particular area will be in the finished print. Conversely, the lighter an area appears on the plate the darker it will be on the finished print.

As mentioned previously this procedure should be carried out in a still bath of ferric chloride. The air pump could be used to produce different results.

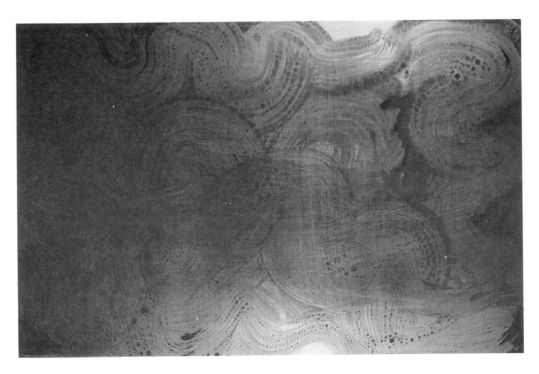

Above: An example of a plate that had the diluted Hunt Speedball Water Soluble Screen Filler number 4570 painted onto the surface.

Above: An example of a print pulled from the plate illustrated at the top of the page. The plate was etched for 3 hours in a 42 Baume mixture of ferric chloride.

Hand Colouring the Etching

One method involves adding colour directly by painting watercolour onto the surface of the etching.

Materials

1. Watercolours.

2. Watercolour brushes.

3. Blotting paper.

4. Container of water.

Watercolour Painting Technique

This method can be used on any etching that has some exposed paper, and is ideal for colouring etchings that have been made with a halftone image.

Below: The halftone etching is made up of a series of small inked dots printed onto clean paper. If a brush is charged with watercolour and brushed onto the surface of the halftone etching, the watercolour will easily be absorbed by the paper and be resisted by the particles of ink.

The watercolour, that was resisted by the ink, will bead and is best removed by laying down blotting paper.

Hand colouring is best achieved one colour at a time, blotting each colour as quickly as possible.

If colour is accidentally splashed in an unwanted area, immediately charge a clean brush with water and douse the splashed colour and blot. Another method of removing unwanted dried paint is to use Scotch Tape (see page 86).

Inking One Plate with Different Colours

Another simple method of applying colour is to selectively add coloured ink to areas of the plate and print it. This method is commonly known as *a la poupee* or selective wiping.

The Technique of Selective Wiping

Small pieces of card corresponding to the size of each area to be wiped are used to lay down the various coloured etching ink.

The wiping of these plates can be carried out in two ways:

1. Each colour can be inked and wiped separately.

2. All the coloured inks can be inked in succession and then wiped.

The latter technique causes the colours to mix and blend together more so than the first.

Using multiple colour plates is another method of colour printing. (Further information about multicolour printing can be sought through reading other printmaking books listed in the "Selected Reading" section page 106.)

Reworking the Plate

There are several techniques that allow the image on the plate to be altered. Although a halftone image may have been used, it is sometimes necessary to lighten or darken certain parts of this image. This can be done in one of the following ways:

1. Recoating and re-etching the plate.

2. Without re-etching, by removing and smoothing out the plate.

3. Adding lines and areas with dry-point or by using engraving tools.

Making the Etched Plate Lighter

If an area on the plate needs to be lightened, a scraper and burnisher can be used depending on how deeply bitten this area is.

Below: The burnisher and scraper are small hand tools. The scraper is best described as a pointed triangular shaped chisel and the burnisher is a similar shaped tool with a pointed end and no sharp edges.

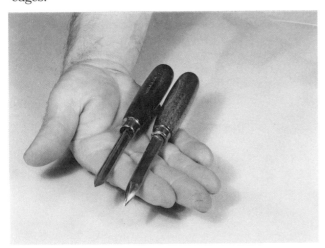

Generally the scraper is not used by itself. It is used to remove deeply bitten lines or tonal areas, after which the marks made by the scraper are smoothed out by the burnisher.

Some shallow marks can be smoothed out directly with the burnisher.

Using the Burnisher and Scraper

Below: A drop of lightweight oil is always placed onto the area to be burnished or scraped. The methods of using both implements are much the same. The burnisher is held in one hand, with guidance and pressure exerted by the thumb and fingers of the other hand.

Another Method of Lightening Areas

Selective "open-biting" of the plate in the unwanted dark areas can lighten these areas. Parts of the plate that require no further etching will have to be blocked out with Hunt Speedball Water Soluble Screen Filler. After these areas have been blocked out, seal the back of the plate with liquid acrylic floor finish and drop it into a bath of ferric chloride. After 30 minutes there will be a noticeable difference. The longer it stays in the ferric chloride the lighter it will get.

Another Method of Darkening Areas

Areas or lines can be scratched deeply into the copper with engraving tools or dry-point needle.

Below: Engraving tools are v-shaped tools that are designed to cleanly cut into metal.

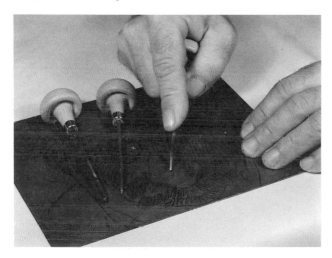

Below: Dry-point needles are designed to scratch into the metal, creating a burr that results in a 'velvety' black line in the finished print.

Both of the above methods can be used to darken areas or lines.

Below: Another method, that is often ignored, is the use of an inexpensive electric engraver (the type used to write names onto tools etc.). Electric engravers have a tungsten point that vibrates and creates a stippling effect. On some models this vibrating point has a variable control.

The Mezzotint

The mezzotint is an intaglio printing technique where the plate is given a random texture similar to a piece of sand paper. To achieve a gradation of tones the plate is burnished and scraped, and the more polished the surface, the whiter it will appear in the finished print.

There are many books that give an ample description of this process. (See "Selected Reading" page 106.)

Recycling Your Plates

When you have completely finished with both sides of your copper plates take them to the scrap metal dealer and cash them in. You may be surprised how much they are worth.

Removing Plate Tone and Fine Scratches

Traditionally, plate tone and fine scratches were removed by arduously polishing and burnishing. Now there is a far easier method, which simply involves **degreasing** (page 32) and coating the final etched plate with clear acrylic floor polish.

The plate is held upright in a photo tray, and the clear floor polish is poured from the top of the plate and allowed to flow over the plate, creating an even coating. This is the identical procedure as demonstrated on page 73 "Applying the Hard-ground".

The plate is left to dry without the aid of a fan. Once dry it forms a very smooth, glass-like finish that fills in very fine scratches and provides a surface that allows ink to be wiped away cleanly.

Below: Transferring a drawing to a hard-ground coated plate can easily be accomplished by rubbing chalk onto the back of the drawing and pressing it through onto the plate with a pencil. (Use the powdered chalk designed for "snap-down" chalk lines.)

1. **Below:** Print showing plate tone.

2. **Below:** The print after the plate had been treated with acrylic floor finish to remove plate tone.

Finishing the Print

Cleaning Up Unwanted Marks

One positive aspect about using good quality rag paper is the ease with which unwanted marks can be removed.

Some pencil and smudge marks can be easily removed by a good pencil eraser.

Ink and watercolour marks are best removed with Scotch Tape. The best way to remove an ink mark, about the size of the end of a pencil, is to lay over about 4" of tape. Gently apply pressure to the back of the tape with your finger and as you get closer to the ink blob, apply more pressure. The tape is then pulled back on itself rapidly. If this is done correctly, only a fraction of the ink mark will be removed. The aim is to remove only a small amount of ink laden paper with each application until the ink is completely gone. After the ink has been completely removed, the actual texture of the paper will be disturbed, and this can be smoothed down by applying a circular rubbing motion with the back of a finger nail. With this method, most marks will disappear without a trace.

Above: Pulling the tape back on itself, removing only a small amount of the ink laden paper with each application.

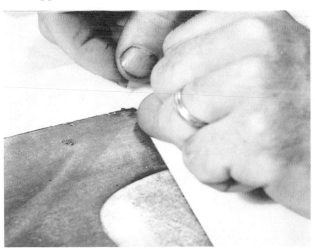

Above: Rubbing the tape down with the thumb.

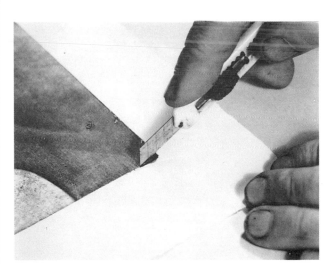

Above: When removing an ink bleed from the perimeter of the image a sharp knife should first lightly cut in the direction of the plate edge. This will ensure a clean edge when the ink mark is removed.

Signing and Titling the Print

It is customary for printmakers to sign their prints in pencil. This is primarily an aesthetic judgement based on the premise that pencil is a more harmonious medium when combined with the medium of original prints.

When producing a limited edition original print there should be some indication of how limited the edition is. This is usually done in the left hand corner, (although I am sure it could be done elsewhere) by penciling in a number that looks like a fraction. The bottom number indicates how many prints are in the edition, or will eventually be made. The top number is a way for individualizing each print. It does not actually mean that the edition was purposely sequenced.

If the letters AP appear instead of the edition number, this means Artist Proof and refers to the prints retained by the artist.

Some artists title their print directly below the printed image and in the center. Titles are also enclosed with inverted commas.

The artist's signature lies at the bottom right, just below the printed image.

Finally, the year the work was produced sometimes follows the signature. Some artists prefer to leave the year of production off as they feel this may prejudice their chance of selling it in the future.

The above method of "signing off" prints basically outlines only one present convention.

Above: Signing the print.

Health and Safety

Since I began promoting health and safety issues in printmaking I have heard many stories about printmakers who have suffered debilitating health damage from exposure to the chemicals and acids of printmaking. To this day, I am still amazed by the number of artists and art teaching institutions that promote the use of KPR and its developer and who are still using nitric acid to etch their plates.

Saying a process is safe is one thing; proving it is another. In an attempt to get some concrete proof of the safety of the "Howard Process", the Alberta Occupational Health and Safety Department (a Canadian Government body) was contacted to do a complete test. On February 13, 1990, Occupational Hygienist Mr. Bill Wong, of their Edmonton office, accompanied by Occupational Hygienists David Doyle and Garfield Colquhoun, of their Grande Prairie office, ran a complete test of the "Howard Process" which employed the mild potassium dichromate sensitizer.

The Major Health Issue

Most of the products used in the "Howard Process" are non-toxic. The greatest concern is the chemicals potassium and ammonium dichromate used as the sensitizing agent. These chemicals in their undiluted state are very toxic (ingestion of as little as 5 grams **(1/5 Oz.)** can cause death) and proper storage and handling must be followed. If these chemicals are to be used by school art teachers I would recommend that they are safely stored in lock-up cabinets in the Science Department chemical storage areas or in some area accessible **only** by the art teacher. Furthermore I recommend that the art teacher be completely responsible for making up the sensitizing solution and that the safety precautions outlined on page 23 be strictly followed.

Testing Procedure

When potassium dichromate is mixed with the gelatin and sprayed onto the etching plate, the potassium dichromate in this mist is referred to as *hexavalent chromium* mist. The methodology of testing has been directly quoted from the original test report.

"Airborne hexavalent chromium mists created from the gelatin spray coating process were the major concerns during this occupational hygiene investigation. For the evaluation of the worker exposed to chromium mists in the air, personal (breathing zone) and area samples were taken during the survey. Personal sampling was carried out by placing a sample collecting unit within several inches of the worker's nose. This ensured collection of air that was most likely inhaled by the worker during the work process. Area samples were collected a few feet away from the spraying area."

Final Analysis

The overspray from the gelatin solution was tested by spraying in an unvented spray booth non stop for 2.5 hours. The actual test report is as follows:

"Airborne chromium mists were collected during the spray coating carried out in a small wooden trough located at a fine art studio of the North Peace Adult Education Consortium. The data provided indicates that the concentration of chromium mist on the personal sample during the day of the sampling was within the acceptable limit. The concentrations of chromium mist on the area samples were below detection limits of the analytical method.

The Alberta 8 hour Occupational Exposure Limit for hexavalent chromium (as Cr) water soluble is 0.05 k/m to the power of 3. The results indicate that the concentrations of chromium, on the day of the sampling, were well below the exposure limit."

In fact, the personal sampling under the above conditions, proved to be **fifty times lower than the Occupational Exposure Limit.** There was not enough chromium mist in the air for the area sampling units to detect. These units were placed 3, 6 and 10 feet away from the spray booth.

It should be reiterated that the spray booth had no exhaust or any other ventilation on it, allowing for "a worst case scenario".

Other Chemicals

Many of the products used in this book are common consumable goods with the exception of the etchant, ferric chloride and the sensitizing agents potassium and ammonium dichromate. If the mixing instructions and advice are followed, there should be little concern with endangering your health. Both ferric chloride and the dichromates have a natural built in safety barrier because of their powerful staining power. If skin comes into direct contact with these liquids it stains in a similar way that nicotine stains the fingers of heavy smokers.

The prepared gelatin emulsion also has a natural safety barrier because of the addition of blue food colouring, and skin that comes into contact with it will turn blue.

I cannot over emphasize the need to exercise **special precautions** when storing the potassium and ammonium dichromate powders, the stock sensitizing solution and the sensitized gelatin solution. If there is **any** chance that a child may come into contact with these chemicals then put them in a place where it would be impossible for the child to get them. **Do not discard the sensitized gelatin in the garbage bin, because** to a child this looks and feels like jello. Contact your local Government Occupational Health and Safety Officer for proper disposal instructions.

Final Recommendations

In the final analysis the responsibility is on every person involved in printmaking activities to control the contaminants created in the studio.

Local ventilation, such as fume hoods, would aid in reducing airborne contaminants further.

Personal protective equipment such as appropriate gloves, apron, respirator and safety goggles should provide adequate protection against any of the chemicals used in this book.

It is also recommended that the fish tank heater be inspected by a trained electrician since its application and use, as outlined in this book, are more than its normal demand.

It is the responsibility of printmakers to familiarize themselves with any existing Occupational Health and Safety Legislation that may apply to their worksite especially in regard to disposal of hazardous goods and to implement any safety precautions or hazardous goods disposal pertaining to that legislation.

Wendy Simon: Triptych 9.5" x 4", utilizing the "Howard Process". The first image was made from an 85 line halftone screen and the second images were made directly from a high contrast Kodalith positive.

Trouble-Shooting

Making the Halftone

When making a halftone it is important to remember to follow the directions given. Any deviation whatsoever can result in unacceptable results.

The main controlling factors that determine success are as follows:

1. The lith film and developers must be fresh. If they are not fresh the film will take an unusually long time to develop.

2. **A red safe-light must be used.** If any other light is used it will result in fogging or slightly exposing the film.

3. Every procedure must be scrupulously timed. Test strips are an important aspect of making good halftones and accurate tests lead to identically finished halftones.

4. Use the two part lith developer for a maximum of 30 minutes. Lith film loses its predictability after this amount of time. The film will still develop, but the amount of time needed to fully develop it will progressively get longer and longer. Do not make the mistake of trying to determine when the lith film has an acceptable exposure by watching it develop in the tray. This determination should be made with the magnifier at the end of the develop and fix cycle. It is best to keep an eye on the darkroom timer rather than the lith film during development.

5. If white powdery marks appear on the finished lith film it probably was not fixed properly.

6. If the halftone dot is soft and lacking edge definition, the lith film was not exposed long enough or there was lack of contact between the halftone screen and the lith film.

7. If the halftone dot fills in, the film was exposed too long.

8. If the halftone dot is too transparent, the lith film will need a longer exposure.

Plate Preparation

Below: If the plate has the slightest grease spot on it, either through touching it directly without rubber gloves or not thoroughly cleaning it, the gelatin emulsion will lift. Run water over the entire surface of the plate. If there is a grease spot the water will bead.

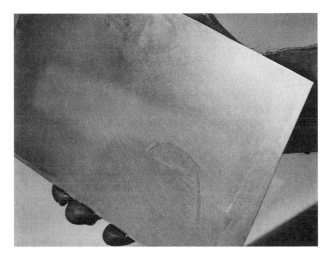

Other problems occur if there is the slightest residue left from the cleaning process. Grit or Comet powder will hamper even distribution of the gelatin.

Applying the Gelatin Emulsion

The first major problem that can be encountered is bubbles in the emulsion. Bubbles can be avoided in two ways:

First, when making the gelatin emulsion, do not mix it vigorously. Let it stand for at least two hours before using.

Second, when transferring the gelatin to the dip-coating tray, do so by bringing the holding container close to the tray and pouring slowly.

Adding a bottle of *Pelican India Ink for fountain pens* helps reduce the amount of surface bubbles and promotes a more even flow of gelatin across the plate.

When dip-coating the plate, the type of latex gloves used is important. Loose fitting gloves will hamper the even distribution of the gelatin at the edges of the plate. Universal stretch fitting latex gloves that hospitals use are best.

Problems arise if the gelatin in the photo tray cools below 100°F. If this happens, the gelatin coating will be uneven and too thick. It is best to do only a few plates at a time, or to use several submersible aquarium heaters to heat the water that surrounds the gelatin-holding tray. If the latter system is employed, it is also a good idea to have a plexiglass lid to cover the gelatin and the surrounding water.

If highly polished copper is used, there may not be enough surface tension to allow the gelatin to flow over the plate without separating. It reacts as if a drop of oil was placed on the surface of the wet gelatin. There must be some tooth on the plate for the gelatin to cling to.

Fan drying the gelatin-coating can cause problems if there are loose particles of dust or lint in the air. These particles can be blown onto the surface of the wet gelatin. If this is an unavoidable problem, the plates can be dried without a fan.

Make sure the gelatin-coated plate is thoroughly dry before using.

As the sensitized gelatin coated plate is sensitive to any source of ultraviolet light, the plates should be prepared and used in subdued light only, and should be stored in a dark cupboard.

The level of subdued light in the studio can be tested by leaving a sensitized plate face up for 10 minutes, covering it periodically in segments, and finally washing out in hot water.

If the segment exposed for ten minutes washes away and the next segments do not, then the studio has a safe exposure factor of ten minutes, as long as conditions remain constant.

If, for some reason, the plate is slightly over-exposed to stray room light it will not fully develop. In a fully developed plate, the raw underlying copper will be visible. In a plate that has been "burnt", the copper will be covered with a thin film of gelatin.

If the gelatin emulsion is left "cooking" in the double boiler for more then 6 weeks it can result in an emulsion that will not develop fully. When I first encountered this problem I had just prepared 7 plates. I exposed each one and etched as normal but each time the final print lost all the fine grays. The smaller dots in the emulsion had filled in. The problem was completely corrected when a new batch of gelatin emulsion was made up.

Remember that the gelatin emulsion should be made up with **distilled water.**

Spray Coating the Gelatin Emulsion

The plate is prepared as with the dip coating method. Most problems arise with the type of air brush used and the method of layering the emulsion onto the plate.

Air brushes that use internal needles to adjust the flow of liquid through the spray nozzle have a tendency to clog up, requiring constant cleaning. Air brushes that use a vacuum system to force the liquid directly through the spray nozzle work extremely well.

Below: Paache air brush model H is the one of the least expensive models and works well.

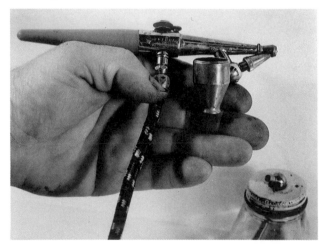

Exposing the Plate

If there is insufficient vacuum created in the vacuum bed, the exposing light will bleed into those areas that should be covered with the halftone screen. To get better contact between the halftone and the plate, the vacuum could be left on for at least 5 minutes before exposure, or a piece of card could be placed at the back of the plate to create additional force between the halftone and the plate.

In the wet method of exposure, problems may occur if the plate is soaked too long in the pre-soaking water bath. If this happens the gelatin may be inadvertently pulled off when the stencil is removed. This may also occur if the stencil is not removed under water. If the positive is damaged or dirt particles are trapped between the lith film positive and the plate, preventing good contact, it will result in dark over exposed marks appearing.

Under and Over-Exposure

Although the exposure latitude of the plate is large, it still can be over or under-exposed.

If, after exposure, the image almost washes away, the plate is under-exposed. Some halftones have a very fine dot structure in the darkest areas. If these areas are under-exposed they may wash away slightly. Sometimes this can be a little hard to detect as the rest of the plate looks normal, but if the plate is held at an acute angle to the light, the washed away emulsion is easily detected. The solution to this problem is to increase the exposure.

Over-exposure can be detected by examining the dot structure on the plate with the pocket magnifier. If the dots start to fill in, then over-exposure has occurred. To remedy this, reduce the exposure.

Developing the Plate

Developing problems will occur if the water temperature is over 120°F or under 110°F.

Be careful when developing the plate that the emulsion is not scratched as it is very fragile, and that the plate is developed for at least 5 minutes. Problems can occur if the unexposed gelatin emulsion is not thoroughly and evenly removed in the water development stage.

Etching the Plate

One of the most critical aspects of the etching process is to constantly monitor the specific gravity (density of the liquid) with a hydrometer. If the specific gravity falls below 42 Baume, the emulsion **will swell and separate from the plate.** This can be easily seen. If the plate did not receive enough UV exposure the same thing may occur. If this problem occurs, increase UV exposure or add more ferric chloride powder to the etchant. If the emulsion continues to lift, the atmospheric humidity in your studio may be too high. In which case pre-soak the plate in a solution of alcohol and water. It is best to make a test plate to see which is the optimum soaking time.

If the plate is not agitated, air bubbles may occur on the surface, preventing the plate from being etched under the bubbles. The plate, at the beginning, should be submerged several times in the ferric chloride and should also be inspected several times during etching. Using the air pump should solve this problem.

As the ferric chloride gets old it loses its etching strength and an oily sludge floats to the surface. If the plate picks up this sludge, retardation of the etching process will occur.

Hydrometers from different manufacturers can give different readings. This may also present a potential problem. To check the reliability of a hydrometer, drop it into a pail of water. If it is accurate the hydrometer will have a reading at the water level of zero.

Most of the experimenting that I have done has occurred in a controlled studio environment of about 70°F. In the summer my studio reached temperatures of up to 85°F and this affected the etching process. When the temperature of the ferric chloride reached about 80°F it had a tendency to etch the plate quicker and to lift the emulsion. This was soon brought under control by using the aquarium air pump outlined on page 60. This had the additional benefit in etching the plate with a finer edge definition. This was due to the constant air bubble flow over the surface of the plate dislodging most of the iron residue formed in the lines during etching.

Fingerprints on the surface of the etching plate, prior to etching, can also retard the etching process.

When using the vertical etching tank, make sure the surface of the plate to be etched is not in contact with the wall of the tank.

Pitting of the plate surface is another problem that occurs if there is 'free acid' present in the ferric chloride solution. This problem generally occurs when tap water is used instead of distilled water in preparing the sensitizing solution, the gelatin solution and the ferric chloride.

If the sensitized plates are etched in a studio that has a low relative humidity the plate will appear to have developed perfectly but will not etch. The reason it will not etch is because an almost invisible film of gelatin will cling to the plate effectively sealing it from the ferric chloride. The simple solution is to hose the plate down with cold tap water and re-etch the plate.

Another exposure problem may arise if the potassium dichromate or ammonium dichromate crystals oxidize. Oxidation occurs when these dichromate crystals and sensitizing solution are left exposed to oxygen for too long. When ordering the dichromate crystals it is a good idea to request crystals **manufactured in the year of purchase.**

If the sensitized gelatin coated plate is left for more than a few weeks without being used it will eventually expose itself. This is referred to as the "dark reaction" and relates to the "shelf life" of this photo-sensitive plate. All light sensitive photo products have a "shelf life" and are susceptible to fogging or exposure if placed in a heated area for too long. These sensitized plates are also susceptible to both time and heat so refrigerated storage is recommended.

The Heated Gelatin Emulsion

This emulsion is light and heat sensitive, and as such, can only be heated continuously for a period of approximately five weeks. After this time the emulsion loses its sensitivity and reacts on a plate as though it was over-exposed. When this happens discard the gelatin and mix up a new batch.

To maximize the life of the gelatin emulsion, keep the double boiler in subdued light.

Printing the Plate

At first glance, the printing procedure may seem simple enough but indeed requires a specialized touch. Between what is considered to be an under and over-wiped plate, there is a range of different acceptable results.

Experienced printmakers develop a preference for a particular brand of ink. Each brand of ink offers a different degree of subtlety, whether it be oily, stiff, or rich in pigment. Inks also have their respective additives that can make them easier to wipe or more transparent. These are individual preferences that new printmakers will have to discover for themselves.

The Printing Paper

The paper must be dampened before use. If the paper is too damp or too dry, the ink will not transfer to the paper successfully. If the paper is too wet, when held at an acute angle to the light, shiny pools of water will be seen. The best test to determine if the paper is too dry is by touch.

Each paper has different absorbency rates. Some papers need only a brief dunking in the water bath, after which they can be hung to dry to the right level of dampness and used without blotting for the final printing. Other papers may need a longer soaking time and blotting procedure. B.F.K Rives is one of the better papers for etching.

Above, Etching, 3" x 3" by **Wendy Simon.**

Aquatinting

No matter what method of aquatint is used, because the etchant is water soluble, the plate must be thoroughly degreased. Greasy marks will hamper the etching process.

When using any of the spray aquatint methods the main problem is either under or overspraying the plate. After the plate has been sprayed and is dry, examine the dot structure with the pocket magnifier (after the emulsion is dry). If the dots start to merge too much, this indicates an overspray. If the dots have too much metal between them, this will indicate an underspray.

Hand Colouring the Etching

The main problem with hand colouring water colours occurs when the plate is insufficiently wiped. If a slight ink residue remains on the surface of the plate, it will resist the water based colour placed on top.

The Hard-Ground

If the acrylic floor finish is applied too thickly, the surface may fracture.

If not enough acrylic floor finish is applied, the plate will have pin hole bites all over it. Sometimes it may be necessary to coat the plate twice, reversing the direction of the coating flow between coats.

The Soft-Ground Substitute

In the "pencil onto tracing paper method", if the pencil mark is too faint it will not print. One method to ensure dense pencil marks is to place a piece of 150 grit wet and dry sand paper directly under the paper where you intend drawing. The texture of this sandpaper will be transposed directly into the pencil line.

Above: A professional drying rack is a great space saver and very convenient when drying prints. If you are looking for a supplier for this type of drying rack consult your telephone directory under "Screen Printing Equipment or Suppliers" or check the Dick Blick art supply catalogue.

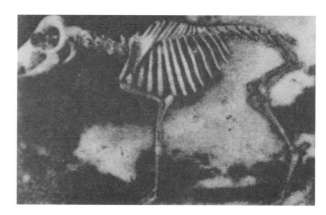

Above, Photo etching, 2 1/2" x 2". This image is a detail from a experimental plate made by Alan Mann at the "Howard Process" workshop conducted at the Australian Print Workshop, Melbourne, Australia.

Sources of Supplies

Printing the actual addresses of suppliers may be helpful in tracking down sources of supply at the time this book was written but times and suppliers change. In addition to listing some suppliers I will be giving a method of tracking down current suppliers in whatever country you may be reading this book. I will be discussing sources of supplies in the order that they appear in this book under the various sectional headings.

What is a Halftone Photograph ?
The Darkroom Setup
How to Make the Perfect Halftone
Alternate Lith Film Processes

Under the above headings the following materials are listed;

1. *The 85 line elliptical dot halftone screen.*
2. *Lith film and lith film developer.*

The 85 line elliptical dot screen are stocked or can be ordered through your local photographic supply store. Generally the stores that sell the lith film will also sell the halftone screens.

The *lith film and developer* are specialized graphic arts products and most of the large photographic film manufacturers produce their own respective brands. For example, Kodak's lith film is called Kodalith, Ilford's lith film is called Ilfolith, Dupont's lith film is called Cronalith or Northern Line Film and Fuji call their lith film Fujilith. They vary in price and quality and they will all work well for the "Howard Process". Each of these respective film manufacturing companies make their own brand of lith developer for their lith films. Retail suppliers for these graphic arts films can be found by either contacting the graphic arts sales manager of these respective companies or by contacting your local photographic supplier. Any current issue of "Popular Photography" will have listed many mail order photographic suppliers.

The supplies listed under "**The Darkroom Setup**" can be found in most retail photographic supply stores. For a listing of mail order photographic stores check the current issue of "Popular Photography".

The *30X Micronta pocket microscope* is available through an electronic store that has many branches in Canada called **Radio Shack** (Radio Shack's catalogue number is 63-851.) Your local high school science teacher may have science supply catalogues that will list a supplier closer to you.

The North American suppliers for the *Micronta 30X microscope* are as follows:

Northwest Laboratories Ltd.
P.O Box 6100, Station C
Victoria,
B C   V8P 5L4
Canada
Phone (604) 592-2434
Toll Free; 1-800-663-5890
(Microscope cat. number 09-0505.)

Northwest Laboratories Ltd
P.O. Box 1356,
Guelph,
Ontario   N1H 6N8
Canada
Phone (519) 836-7720
Toll Free; 1-800-265-7250
(Microscope cat. number 09-0505.)

Northwest Laboratories Inc.
20-255 Great Arrow Drive
Buffalo,
New York   14207
U.S.A.
Phone (716) 877-4748

Northwest Scientific Company Inc.
Box 305
Rocklin,
California   95677
U.S.A.
Phone (916) 652-9229
Fax (916) 652-9672

Boreal Laboratories Ltd.
1820 Mattawa Ave.
Mississauga,
Ontario   L4X 1K6
Canada
Toll Free; 1-800-387-9393
Fax (416) 279-9203
(Microscope cat. number 69989.)

Ward's Natural Science Ltd.
1840 Mattawa Ave.
Mississauga,
Ontario L4X 1K1
Canada
Phone (416) 279-4482
Toll Free; 1-800-387-7822
(Microscope cat. number 25 W 4995.)

There is an *alternate 30X microscope,*
catalogue number S-481747-01 available from;
Sargent-Welch in the following 7 locations:

1. 285 Gary Drive
   Weston,
   Ontario M9L 1P3
   Canada
   Phone (416) 741-5210
   Toll free in Ontario; 1 800-268-5973

2. 3300 Blv. Cavendish
   Montreal,
   Quebec H4B 2M8
   Canada
   Phone (514) 481-0119

3. 7300 North Linder Ave.
   Skokie,
   Illinois 60077
   U.S.A.
   Phone (312) 676-0172
   This is also where the **International Division**
   office is located for orders outside Canada and
   the U.S.A.
   CABLE SARWELSCI
   TELEX 72-4442 or 210049 (RCA)
   Answer Back SWSCI UR
   TWX 910-223-4541
   Telefax: 312-677-4869

4. 3403 Century Circle
   Irving, P.O. Box 152008
   Texas 75015-2008
   U.S.A.
   Phone (214) 579-9200
   800-527-5111
   In Texas; 800-492-4210

5. 3125 Seventh Ave North
   Birmingham, P.O. Box 10404
   Alabama 35202
   U.S.A.
   Phone (205) 251-5125
   800-633-6990
   In Alabama; 800-323-9032

6. 35 Stern Ave.
   Springfield
   New Jersey 07081
   Phone (201) 376-7050
   800-SARGENT

7. 1617 East Ball Rd.
   Anaheim,
   California 92803
   U.S.A.
   (714) 772-355
   800-SARGENT

Another suitable pocket microscope catalogue
number 60-2400 **10X Miniscope** can be
purchased from;

Carolina Biological Supply Company
Main office and laboratories
Burlington,
North Carolina 27215
U.S.A.
Phone (919) 584-0381

Powel Laboratories Division
Gladstone,
Oregon 97027
U.S.A.
Phone (503) 656-1641

The Stock Sensitizing Solution

*Potassium and ammonium dichromate and
distilled water* are the main supplies needed
under this section. When searching out sources
of supply for potassium or ammonium
dichromate a good place to start is the
telephone book under "Chemicals". If one
company does not carry the product then ask
them to direct you to someone who does. The
second source is the local high school, college
or university science teacher. Most science
teachers have an assortment of chemical
catalogues that will list potassium and
ammonium dichromate in them under
"Chemicals and Reagents". I suggest that you
shop around as prices for most items vary.

Latex Exam Gloves can be purchased from:
Canadian International Distributers
8 Dynamic Drive, Suite 8
Scarborough
Ontario M1V 4C8
Canada
Phone (416) 299-8649   or   1-800-668-4352

Some of the chemical companies that stock *potassium and ammonium dichromate* are:

Central Scientific Company of Canada Ltd.
1830 Mattawa Ave.
Mississauga,
Ontario L4X 1K1
Canada
Phone (416) 279-3400
Toll Free; 1-800-268-4355
(*Potassium dichromate* cat. number 38396-95)

Fischer Scientific
Educational Materials
P.O. Box 9200, Terminal
Ottawa,
Ontario K1G 4A9
Phone (613) 228-0542
Toll Free in Canada; 1-800-267-3556
Fax (613) 226-1296
(*Potassium dichromate* catalogue number P186B-500.)

Northwest Laboratories Ltd.
Address listed on page 95. (*Potassium dichromate* cat. number 80-7618-4.)

Ward's Natural Science Ltd.
Address listed on page 96. (*Potassium dichromate* cat. number 39 W 8138.)

Boreal Laboratories Ltd.
Address listed on page 95. (*Potassium dichromate* cat. number 85290-95.)

Sargent-Welch
Address listed on page 96. (*Potassium dichromate* catalogue number C14160-500GM CAS Reg. 7778-50-9.)

Carolina Biological Supply Company
Address listed on page 96. (*Potassium dichromate)* cat. number 88-3200

Distilled water can be purchased from most pharmacies or supermarkets. Sometimes a cheaper source of distilled water can be purchased from those companies that sell water distillers. Generally if you bring your own containers in they will fill them for a nominal charge.

Making the Double Boiler

The *8" Radiant Aquarium Heater with thermostat control* is manufactured by:

Rolf C. Hagen (U.S.A.)
50 Hampden Rd.
Mansfield,
Ma. 02048
U.S.A.

Rolf C. Hagen Inc.
3225 Sartelon St.
Montreal,
Quebec H4R 1E8
Canada

This *8" Radiant Aquarium Heater* is one of the most popular brands used in North America and is generally available from your local pet supply store.

The 3 gallon ice cream bucket can be picked up either for a nominal charge or for free from your local ice cream vendor or any fast food store that sells ice cream. Small plastic storage buckets or plastic garbage bins can be easily substituted for the ice cream container.

The 4 gallon or 16 litre cooking oil container can be found at almost any restaurant. Most restaurants go through many of these containers a week and the restaurant owner is generally more than happy to give them away.

Preparing the Gelatin Emulsion

Knox Unflavoured Gelatine is available in most supermarkets and food stores.

Food Club blue food colouring is also commonly available in food stores and supermarkets.

This particular brand of food colouring is distributed by:

Scott-Bathgate Ltd.
116A Galaxy Blv.
Rexdale,
Ontario M9W 4Y6
Canada
Phone (416) 674-0214

Scott-Bathgate
1050 Hamilton St.
Vancouver
B.C V6B 2R9
Canada
Phone (604) 685-0371

Scott-Bathgate
14425 - 124 Ave.
Edmonton,
Alberta T5L 3B2
Canada
Phone (403) 451-1125

This food colouring is unquestionably the best. Other brands of food colouring reduces the surface tension of the gelatin making it impossible to evenly coat a plate. Some water soluble blue dyes, ink or watercolour may be substituted. I have added a 2 ounce bottle of blue fountain pen ink to the 1 litre (approx. 1 quart) batch of sensitized gelatin solution and it works well although the staining power of this ink is only very slight. (*Please note that the "Howard Process" has only been tested for safety with the Food Club colouring .*)

The 1 litre or 1 quart measuring containers can be purchased through any of the science chemical companies previously listed. Photographic supply stores also have these containers.

Preparing the Copper Plate

The 16 ounce (.022) roofing copper. The best source of supply can be found in the telephone book under "Metals, Copper". Some Canadian suppliers are as follows:

Ideal Metal & Alloys of Canada Inc.
4375-14th St. N.E.
Calgary,
Alberta T2E 7A9
Canada

Drummond McCAll Inc.
2003 91 Ave.
P.O. Box 8547 Station F
Calgary,
Alberta P2J 2V6
Canada
Phone (403) 467-0637

A & M Non-Ferrous Metals
12311 Horseshoe Way
Richmond,
B C V78 4S5
Canada
Phone (604) 272-24422

Copracan Industries Ltd.
4062 McConnell Dr.
Burnaby,
B C V58 3A8
Canada
Phone (604) 421-3493

Two alternate grades of copper that are thicker and better in quality are; industrial *copper plates for etchers* and *polished copper plates for etchers,* available from:

Daniel Smith Inc.
4130 First Ave. South
Seattle,
Washington 98134
U.S.A.
Toll free 1 800 426-6740
Customer service 1-800-426-7923
In WA: 1-800-228-0458

Three more alternate grades of copper; Engravers, 16 gauge economy and 18 gauge economy are available from:

Graphic Chemical & Ink Co.
P.O. Box 27
728 North Yale Ave.
Villa Park,
Illinois 60181
U.S.A.
Phone (312) 832-6004

Dick Blick Art Materials (address next page) catalogue lists two sizes of 16 gauge copper plates:

5" x 7" cat. no. 93605
8" x 10" cat. no. 93608

Dick Blick Art Materials has a mail order catalogue that is one of the most extensive that I have seen and is listed at the following locations:

Dick Blick West
P.O. Box 521
Henderson,
Nevada 89015
U.S.A.
Phone (702) 451-7662
Fax: (702) 451-8196

Dick Blick Central
P.O. Box 1267
Galesburg,
Illinois 61401
U.S.A.
Phone (309) 343-6181
Fax: (309) 343-5785

Dick Blick East
P.O. Box 26
Allentown,
PA 18105
U.S.A.
Phone (215) 965-6051
Fax: (215) 965-4026

A toll free number exists for anywhere in the continental U.S.; weekdays from 8 am. to 4.30 pm., Central Time:

1-800-447-8192,
for customer service call, **1-800-373-7575**

I would recommend contacting Dick Blick to get a copy of their free catalogue and to see if they have a retail store close to your location.

The 320 grit wet and dry sandpaper and electric sander are commonly available through your local hardware store.

The Comet cleanser, pots and pans scrubber pad and dishwashing gloves are available in the local supermarket.

Applying the Gelatin Emulsion

The darkroom thermometer and photo developing trays. available from your local photo supply store. **The Dick Blick** catalogue has in inexpensive tray called "The Super Tub" measuring 30" x 19" and 8" deep listed: Cat. no. 4238100.

The unprinted newsprint . The cheapest way of purchasing this is to go to the local newspaper office and buy newspaper roll ends. Some newspaper offices give roll ends away. The alternative is to buy it at the local art supply store.

The latex surgical gloves. If the local pharmacy does not carry this type of glove try going to your local hospital and purchasing them directly from their store room. Hospitals may allow direct purchases such as this if the product is unavailable in your local pharmacy. Each hospital has its own policy in this regard.

Eye protection glasses and work aprons.. Available through your local hardware or safety supply store or through the **Dick Blick Art Supply** catalogue: Coverflex goggles Cat. no. 747200 and the 3M Easi-Air Paint Spray Respirator Assembly, check the catalogue for the one to suit your face and needs.

The Spray Coating Method

The single action Paasche air brush model H with the medium number 3 nozzle and compressor is available at your local art supply store or mail order through:

Dick Blick Art Supply, cat. no. 1700100. This particular airbrush is also available as a set, cat. no. 1708600.

Daniel Smith Inc. listed on page 98 also has a large selection of alternate air brushes and compressors.

Daniel Smith Inc. also has the following:
The carbon filtered respirator product number 9894010 and replacement cartridge number 9894011.
The SAF Scanner Protective goggles product number 9894018.

The Acetate Roll-up Variation

Acetate can be purchased in roll form from your local art or graphic art supply store or mail ordered from:

Daniel Smith Inc. (address on page 98) product number 8360000.

Check in the **Dick Blick Art Material** catalogue (address page 99) under "Acetate" in the index.

Brayer can be purchased from your local art supply store or mail ordered from:

Daniel Smith Inc. product number 9780066. If a larger roller is desired Daniel Smith Inc. also sells an excellent roller that varies in length from 12" to 32" called the Chameleon Roller.

Check in the **Dick Blick Art Materials** catalogue (address page 99) under "Brayer" in the index.

Exposing and Developing the Plate

The photo tray is listed under "Applying the Gelatin Emulsion" on the previous page.

Large cotton balls. Sometimes referred to as cotton wool is available at your local pharmacy or supermarket.

Rubber gloves. Are available from your local supermarket or pharmacy.

Light source. If fluorescent black lights, full spectrum fluorescent lights or the G.E. Sunlamp are used as the exposure source these are available through your local lighting fixture store. For more elaborate exposure units check your local phone directory under "Screenprinting Supplies" or "Printing Supplies".

Dick Blick Art Materials (address on page 99) has some of the most economical exposure units available listed in their catalogue index under "Screen Printing".

The Etching Tank

For a supplier of *plexiglass and plexiglass glue* check your local telephone directory under "Plastic Products". Companies that sell large quantities of plexiglass will generally cut the plexiglass to order for a minimum charge. Most glaziers and hardware stores also sell plexiglass but generally they will not cut it to order and it is more expensive.

The fiberglass mesh and resin and the silicon sealant glue are available from your local hardware or auto accessory store.

Mixing and Testing the Ferric Chloride

The ferric chloride and heavy liquid hydrometers can be purchased from most of the chemical companies listed in this section.

Avoid purchasing ferric chloride in 500 gms (17.6 oz.) powdered lots as buying it in these small quantities can cost up to 40 times more than purchasing it in larger sizes. The same can be said for the smaller sized liquid quantities of ferric chloride. Shop around for comparative pricing. Most chemical companies that do not have a toll free line will accept collect calls.

Northwest Laboratories Ltd. (address on page 95). *Ferric chloride powder*, technical grade catalogue number 2kg. (4.4 lbs.) 80-4472T-5 *Hydrometer*, double scale approx. 15" in length catalogue number 24-4234

Boreal Laboratories Ltd. (address on page 95) *Hydrometer*, approx. 12" in length, catalogue number 62105.

The electronics industry uses ferric chloride in the production of printed circuit boards. This is an alternate source of supply. Check your local telephone book. Some North American chemical supply companies that sell ferric chloride are:

Cardinal Electronics
10630 172 St.
Edmonton,
Alberta T5S 1H8
Canada
Phone (403) 483-6266
Cardinal Electronics distribute 4 litre bottles (1.05 gal.) that are made by **M.G. Chemicals**, catalogue number 415-4L.

M.G. Chemicals
9347 193 St.
Surry,
B C V3T 4W2
Canada
Phone (604) 888-3084

M.G. Chemicals
80 Hale Rd. Number 13
Brampton,
Ontario L6W 3M1
Canada
Phone (416) 454-4178

One Canadian and U.S. source for bulk ferric chloride powder is Anachemia Science. They sell 135 lb and 22 lb lots of technical grade ferric chloride product number AC-4472T.

Anachemia Science
101- 3820 Jacoms Rd.
Richmond,
B C V6V 1Y6
Canada
Phone (403) 270-2252

Anachemia Science
15018-116 Ave.
Edmonton,
Alberta T5M 3T4
Canada
Phone (403) 451-0665

Anachemia Science
Unit A 3120 Pepper Mill Court
Mississauga,
Ontario L5L 4X4
Canada
Phone (416) 828-9599
Toll Free in Can. 1-800-387-8106

Anachemia Science
2250-46th Ave.
Lachine,
Montreal H8T 2P3
Quebec
Canada
Phone (514) 636-8481

Anachemia Science
1816 Deming Way
Sparks,
Nevada 89431
U.S.A.
Phone (702) 331-2300

One of the cheapest sources of *bulk ferric chloride* is from **Van Waters & Rogers,** a wholesale chemical supply company that have many branches throughout North America. The minimum order size is 60 kilos or 130 lbs. product number 11-26550. Generally they sell to companies, institutions and professional organizations. It could be argued that an artist is in fact a manufacturer and should be entitled to deal directly with this company. To a great degree the sort of reception that you may encounter from this company will depend on the flexibility of their order person. If they are not willing to ship the ferric chloride out collect, then offer to post them a certified check. If this fails at one office call another or try purchasing it through your local printmaking society.

To find the **Van Waters & Rogers** branch closest to you consult your local telephone directory or call one of the following offices:

Canadian Head Office
9800 Van Horne Way
Richmond,
B C V6X 1W5
Canada
Phone (604) 273-1441

Canadian Eastern Office
64 Arrow Rd.
Toronto,
Ontario M9M 2L8
Canada
Phone (416) 741-9190

Eastern Regional Office
Camp Croft Industrial Park, Hwy. 295
Spartenburg
South Carolina 29302
U.S.A.
Phone (803) 596-1800

Central Regional Office
600 Hunter Dr.
Oak Brook 60521-1926
Illinois
U.S.A.
Phone (312) 573-4300

South West Regional Office
10889 Bekay St.
Dallas,
Texas 75238-1313
U.S.A.
Phone (214) 340-7300

Western Region
1363 South Bonnie Beach Place
Los Angeles,
California 90023-4001
U.S.A.
Phone (213) 265-8123

Plate Preparation
Prior to Etching

The roll of Mac Tac can be purchased at your local wallpaper/ paint and hardware store.

The bottle of liquid acrylic floor finish should be available at your local supermarket.

Etching the Plate

The aquarium air pump and plastic tubing is available at your local pet supply store. The plastic tubing can be purchased by the foot in any length needed. The diaphram air pump model Elite 801 is distributed by **Rolf C. Hagen Inc.** (address on page 97.)

The etching needle is available from **Daniel Smith, Inc. , Graphic Chemical & Ink Co.** (address on page 98), and **Dick Blick Art Materials** (address on page 99).

The black electricians tape and pliers are available from your local hardware store

Printing the Plate

Many of the following materials can be purchased from your local art supply store or mail order through the **Graphic Chemical & Ink Co.** (address on page 98), **Daniel Smith Inc.** (address on page 98) and **Dick Blick Art Materials** (address on page 99) and **Praga Industries Co. Ltd.** (a Canadian supplier listed on page 103). All of the above suppliers have extensive art material catalogues. Call them and request a free copy.

Etching Ink   There are many different types of etching inks available. More information about the different types and uses of these inks can be found in the above catalogues or by directly calling the above companies.

Tarlatan

Palette knife

Gloves for inking

Etching paper There are many different papers suitable for etching, the **Daniel Smith** catalogue has one of the best selections and usage description.

Blotting paper

Etching blankets

Anti-skin spray

The etching press is an important consideration if you intend setting up your own etching studio. If you do not want to purchase an etching press, most major cities have printmaking co-operatives that will rent their facilities. Many of these print workshops also offer short courses in etching. One way that you could find out about local print co-operatives is to contact the printmaking staff at your local university or art college. If you intend purchasing an etching press I would advise you to shop around to find the one that suits your pocketbook and needs. Visit your local university Fine Arts Department or art college and see what sort of presses they have and ask the etching instructors for their advice. All the suppliers listed below have a comprehensive catalogue. Write or call them and request a copy.

Dick Blick Art Supplies (address page 99) has some of the <u>most economical presses</u> available. Their **"Econo Etch"** press is excellent for beginners and will manage a print size of up to 9" x 18" (1991, priced under US$300.00). They have three other models, the most expensive being the **"Master Etch"** that delivers a print size of 22" x 34" (1991, priced under US$2,000.00). Call them and request their catalogue. Following are some companies that manufacture or distribute good quality **etching presses:**

Daniel Smith, Inc. (Address listed on page 98.) distributes the **"Ettan Press"**, excellent quality presses that have bed sizes ranging from 12" x 24" to 24 1/2" x 48 3/4". Contact the toll free number listed and request a copy of their "Materials and Information for Artists" catalogue. This catalogue is very comprehensive and informative.

Two Canadian Etching Press manufacturers :
Praga Industries Co. Ltd.
120 Barbados Blvd.
Scarborough,
Ontario M1J 1L2
Canada
Phone (416) 264-3356

Advance Tool and Dye
5616-94A Street
Edmonton,
Alberta T6E 3E4
Canada
Phone (403) 435-2474

Charles Brand
45 York St.
Brooklyn,
New York,
N.Y. 11201
U.S.A.
Phone (718) 797-1887

Takach-Garfield Press Co.
3207 Morningside Drive N.E.
Albuquerque,
New Mexico 87110
U.S.A.
Office (505) 881-8670
Shop (505) 242-7674

Griffin Co.
1745 East 14th St.
Oakland,
California 94606
U.S.A.
Phone (415) 533-0600

Glen Alps
6523 40th Ave NE
Seattle,
Washington 98115
U.S.A.
Phone (206) 523-8754

American French Tool Co.
Route 117
Coventry,
Rhode Isand 02816
U.S.A.
Phone (401) 821-0452

Rembrandt Graphic Arts
The Crane Farm
Rosemont,
New Jersy 08556
U.S.A.
Phone (505) 242-7674

Applied Arts International
22313 Meekland Ave.
Hayward,
California 94541
U.S.A.
Phone (415) 537-9773

Hunter Penrose, Ltd.
7 Spar Rd.
London SE16 3Q3
England

David Gafiss, etching, 9" x 6" made at the "Howard Process" workshop conducted at the Australian Print Workshop, Melbourne, Australia. This etching was made by drawing directly onto the sensitized gelatin emulsion with water soluble ink, exposing, developing and then etching the plate. This image was further worked with the "Screen Filler Lift Ground" and a dry-point needle.

The Aquatint Method

The materials needed in this section are listed on page 97 under "Preparing the Gelatin Emulsion" and under "The Spray Coating Method".

New Approach to Hard and Soft Ground

The materials needed for most of this section can be found on page 102 under "Plate Preparation Prior to Etching".

The Pelican India Ink for fountain pens can be purchased in most stationery or art supply stores.

The water soluble relief-ink is manufactured by the **Graphic Chemical & Ink Co.** listed on page 98. This ink is also available through **Daniel Smith Inc.** listed on the same page.

Printing Intaglio and Relief Together

Materials needed for this section can be found on page 102 under "Plate Preparation Prior to Etching" and on page 100 "Acetate Roll-up Variation".

Screen Filler Lift-Ground

The Hunt Speedball water soluble screen filler 4570 can be purchased through most art supply stores that sell Hunt Speedball products. The **Dick Blick Art Materials** catalogue (page 99) has it listed as "Screen Filler" cat. No. 613906.

A direct enquiry could be made to:

Hunt Manufacturing Co.
Statesville
North Carolina 28677
U.S.A.
Phone (704) 872-9511

Hand Colouring the Etching

The watercolours and watercolour brushes can be purchased at any art supply store or through the **Dick Blick Art Materials** catalogue (page 99) or the **Daniel Smith** catalogue (page 98).

The blotting paper can be purchased at any stationery store or through **Daniel Smith Inc.** product code 8060028 & 29 & 30 or **Dick Blick Art Materials** cat. no. 7059015 & 7749700.

Reworking the Plate

The burnisher, scraper, dry-point needle and mezzotint tools. A number of different types can be purchased from **Daniel Smith Inc.** address on page 98 and the **Graphic Chemical Ink Co.** address on the same page and through the **Dick Blick Art Materials** catalogue (page 99).

The electric engraver can be purchased through the **Dick Blick Art Materials** catalogue and is called the "Dremel Electric Engraver" cat. no. 3336000. These electric type of engravers are also commonly available at most hardware stores along with the *chalk line powder*.

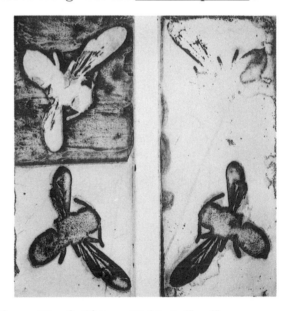

Above: Wendy Simon, Etching, 4" x 4"

Selected Reading

Photography Books

Curtin, Dennis, and Maio, J.C. *The Darkroom Handbook.* Marblehead, M.A: Curtin and London, 1979. Distributed by Focal Press.

Davis, Phil. *Photography*, Dubuque, IA: Wm. C. Brown Publishers, 6th edition 1990.

The Focal Encyclopedia of Photography, New York: McGraw-Hill Company, 1969.

Gassan, Arnold. *A Handbook for Contemporary Photography*, Athens, Ohio: Handbook Co., 1974.

Grill, Tom, and Scanlon, Mark. *The Essential Darkroom Book: A Complete Guide to Black and White and Color Processing*: New York: Amphoto, 1981.

Horenstein, Henry. *Beyond Basic Photography*. Boston: Little, Brown and Co., 1977

Life Library of Photography. New York: Time-Life books, 1970

Ruggles, Joanne and Phillip. *Darkroom Graphics*, Garden City, N.Y. : Amphoto, 1975.

Simon, Michael/Moore, Dennis. *First Lessons in Black-and-White Photography*, New York: Holt. Rinehart and Winston, 1978.

Stone, Jim, ed. *Darkroom Dynamics: A Guide to Creative Darkroom Techniques.* Somerville, MA: Curtin and London, 1979. Distributed by Focal Press.

Swedlund, Charles. *Photography: A Handbook of History, Materials and Processes.* 2nd ed. New York: Holt Rinehart and Winston, 1981.

Upton, Barbara London, with Upton John. *Photography*. 3rd ed. Boston: Little, Brown and Co., 1984

Vestal, David. *The Craft of Photography.* New York: Harper and Row, 1975.

_____, *The Art of Black-and-White Enlarging.* New York: Harper and Row, 1984.

General Printmaking Books

Dawson, John, editor. *The Complete Guide to Prints and Printmaking; History, Materials and Techniques from Woodcut to Lithography*, New York: Quill Publishing, 1981.

Eichenberg, Fritz. *The Art of the Print.* New York: Abrams. 1976.

Hacking, Nicholas/Tinsley, Francis/Turner, Silvie. *Practical Printmaking*, New Jersey: Chartwell Books Inc., 1983.

Hamerton, P.H. *Etchers and Etching*, New York: Macmillan, 1976.

Hayter, Stanley William. *New Ways of Gravure*, London: Oxford University Press, 1966.

Heller, Jules. *Printmaking Today*, New York: Holt. Rinehart and Winston, 1972.

Newman, Thelma R. *Innovative Printmaking: The Making of Two-and Three-Dimensional Prints and Multiples*, New York: Crown Publishers, Inc., 1977.

Melot, Michel/Griffiths, Antony/Field, Richard S./Beguin, Andre. *Prints: History of an Art*, New York: Rizzoli International Publications, 1981.

Rosen, Randy. *Prints: The Facts and Fun of Collecting*, New York: E.P.Dutton, 1978.

Ross, John and Romano, Clare. *The Complete Printmaker*, New York: The Free Press. A division of Macmillan Publishing Co., Inc., 1972.

Sacilotto, Deli. *Photographic Printmaking Techniques,* New York: Watson-Guptill Publications, 1982.

Saff, Donald and Sacilotto, Deli. *Printmaking: History and Process,* New York: Holt, Rinehart and Winston, 1978.

William M., Ivins, Jr. *Prints and Visual Communication*, London, England: M.I.T. Press 5th printing, May 1982.

Index

Your etching wish list
☐ *Yes*

-*I am concerned for my own health.*

-*I want a safer environment in which to work.*

-*I want the option of making etchings safely in my own home.*

-*I want etching techniques to be environmentally friendly.*

-*I want the most inexpensive means of making etchings.*

-*I want techniques that are relatively simple.*

-*I want to be able to easily purchase etching materials.*

-*I want to be a better printmaker.*

Book Re-order Form
Safe Photo Etching for Photographers and Artists
☐ **Yes** I want to share the knowledge

Enclosed is payment of $24.95 (includes G.S.T.) plus $2.95 for postage and handling (sent by Canada Post). Total cost for one book $27.90

Bill my ☐ Visa ☐ Mastercard

Acct. #_____Exp. Date_____

Signature_____

Bank or cashiers check are acceptable. If more than one book is ordered write the number of books ordered_____ and multiply that number by $27.90 to arrive at a total cost. Write total amount $_____

Name_____

Address_____

City_____

Province/State_____

Country_____Postal Code/Zip_____

Enclose this order form in an envelope with payment and send to:
Wynne Resources: P.O. Box 7587
Peace River, Alberta   T8S 1T2   CANADA

Book Re-order Form
Safe Photo Etching for Photographers and Artists
☐ **Yes** I want to share the knowledge

Enclosed is payment of $24.95 (includes G.S.T.) plus $2.95 for postage and handling (sent by Canada Post). Total cost for one book $27.90

Bill my ☐ Visa ☐ Mastercard

Acct. #_____Exp. Date_____

Signature_____

Bank or cashiers check are acceptable. If more than one book is ordered write the number of books ordered_____ and multiply that number by $27.90 to arrive at a total cost. Write total amount $_____

Name_____

Address_____

City_____

Province/State_____

Country_____Postal Code/Zip_____

Enclose this order form in an envelope with payment and send to:
Wynne Resources: P.O. Box 7587
Peace River, Alberta   T8S 1T2   CANADA